Goose River Anthology, 2014

Edited by

Deborah J. Benner

Goose River Press
Waldoboro, Maine

Library of Congress Card Number: 2014913948

ISBN: 978-1-59713-155-1

First Printing, 2014

Cover photo by Diane C. Reitz

Published by
Goose River Press
3400 Friendship Road
Waldoboro ME 04572
e-mail: gooseriverpress@roadrunner.com
www.gooseriverpress.com

Author's Included

Author's Included

In Memory of

Susan Connelly

Herb Coursen

Mollie Schmidt

W.R. Olsen

Philip Pendleton

Goose River Anthology, 2014

Juliana L'Heureux
Topsham, ME

Somewhere in France

No one in the family had visited Uncle Nap's grave in France.

My husband and I traveled by train from Paris to visit the quiet town of Château-Thierry in northeast France. It's a scenic location, so picturesque the panorama is suitable for framing. Complete with a real chateau, the town's charm would likely enchant any casual tourist.

Yet, a century ago, 1914 — 1918, the landscape was embroiled in the Great European War. Château–Thierry's charm today is a veneer for the memories of thousands of people who once lived in terror, surrounded by no-mans-lands, trench warfare and barbed wire barricade fences.

Paradoxically, World War I was supposed to be "the war to end all wars." Instead, it was a prelude to even more horrific events in World War II.

A rapidly dwindling number of people alive today likely know how Château–Thierry's beauty is also the somber location of the 42.5 acre American Veterans Aisne-Marne Cemetery. It's a World War I burial ground, landscaped with the headstones of 2,288 casualties plus 251 unknown. Most of the dead were fatalities from the Battle of Château–Thierry and the Battle of Belleau Woods, in France.

During the fighting after the Battle of Château-Thierry—fought on July 18, 1918—Uncle Napoleon "Nap" Morin, age 19, of Biddeford, Maine, was tragically killed while trying to provide evacuation assistance to wounded soldiers from the American Expeditionary Forces (AEF).

My mother-in-law, Rose Anna, was Nap's sister. She spoke about war with uncharacteristic obscenities throughout her long life. In fact, war made her a pacifist. It's understandable, after she witnessed the tragedy of having her mother receive Nap's death notice, then experiencing the life

Juliana L'Heureux
Topsham, ME

long grief, resulting from the loss of her brother, and subsequently sending three of her own sons to survive World War II, the Korean Conflict, and Viet Nam.

"Somewhere in France" was the heading of the September 21, 1918 dated letter, notifying the family about Nap's death. Although the parchment paper is fragile with age, the message is as chilling to read today, as it was when it was delivered to Mrs. Emma Morin. It's obvious the letter was hand-typed by someone who found spelling and punctuation to be challenging.

"I am writing you relative to the death of your son who was killed in battle on August 8, 1918. The sacrifice he made was among one supreme (*typographical error was marked out here*). 'Greater love hath no man that (sic) this, that a man lay down his life for his friends.' There is comfort in the fact that the value of a person's life does not depend upon its length but its investment. Yours in deep sympathy, Lewis W. Dockery, 1st Lieutenant and Chaplain, 38th Infantry."

Nap was among nine million who were counted among World War I deaths.

Locating the grave of American veterans is the work of the American Battlefield Monuments Commission. A database with every service person buried in a veterans' cemetery is kept by the Commission. We could never have found the Aisne-Marne Cemetery without the detail provided. A few days before leaving for France, a package arrived from the American Battlefield Monuments Commission containing a map of the area we were going to in France, directions for how to locate the cemetery and a picture of the location. Most important, the directions also told us where to look for Uncle Nap's memorial, inside the magnificent rose granite colonnade, right above the religious altar in the chapel. Uncle Nap's name was engraved in the chapel because he was among those who were cremated, rather than buried. Later, we learned that the chapel inside the colonnade was built on the location of the front line trench where Uncle Nap may

Juliana L'Heureux
Topsham, ME

have actually died.

So, we had the directions to Château-Thierry and a picture of what we were looking for, but we still had to find our way to the location of the cemetery.

At the Château-Thierry train station, we were the only two Americans standing on the disembarking platform. Everyone ignored us while we walked to a queue of taxi cabs. To our utter amazement, the first cab driver refused to drive us to the cemetery! He was followed by a second taxi driver, who also refused our fare.

On a third try, I pleaded with the driver about visiting my husband's uncle's grave, but it was obvious, even he didn't want to drive us to the cemetery.

Yet, the third driver looked like he was considering a change of heart.

"C'est l'oncle de mon mari!," je l'ai dit. ("It's my husband's uncle!," I said.)

It worked. We were driven about 20 minutes outside of the town to the cemetery. Other taxi drivers probably didn't want to miss quick turn around fares and lose multiple customers during the time it took to drive to Aisne-Marne, plus wait for us to visit the gravesite. Thankfully, our map showed us exactly where to look for Uncle Nap's name, so we didn't waste time finding the chapel located inside the cemetery's rose granite colonnade.

We were the only two people in the cemetery. It was surreal to be in an American veterans' cemetery with over a thousand headstones and not see another person. A quiet sadness engulfed us as we realized how rare an event it was to be among so many dead. Their ages at death were between 19 and 23 years old. They're eternally young in their graves, while their families of a century ago are too old to visit them anymore.

Although the cemetery was without visitors, at least while we were there, the maintenance of the graves and the lawns was impeccable. Rose bushes lined all the walkways. Inside,

Juliana L'Heureux
Topsham, ME

the chapel was immaculately clean and the granite altar gleamed like polished crystal. We quickly made a pencil rubbing on paper of Corporal Napoleon Morin's name.

Meanwhile, our taxi driver waited with the cab, having refused our offer to go with us while we walked to the chapel. Upon returning, we were excited to show him the pencil rubbing with the name of the deceased person he had driven us to visit. But, I was stunned when he sadly looked at the name and broke down crying! While I was gleeful for having made the pencil drawing of Uncle Nap's name, our driver was appropriately mourning our family's sacrifice to help secure his nation's sovereignty.

Surely, I thought to myself, this taxi driver's family told him stories about what the peaceful Aisne-Marne Cemetery meant to them.

We're grateful for the opportunity to visit the Aisne-Marne Cemetery and for the assistance of the American Battlefield Monuments Commission in helping us to locate Uncle Nap's memorial.

Our regret was in the realization that no one else in the family would ever follow in our footsteps, because Uncle Nap was unmarried when he went to war.

Moreover, those who would have joined us in tears of grateful appreciation (along with the French taxi driver), especially Emma Morin, and Rose Anna Morin L'Heureux and her siblings, are themselves deceased.

It was an unforgettable experience for my husband and me, but when we came back home to Maine, there was no one alive from the immediate family to tell.

Diane H. Schetky
Topsham, ME

Afghanistan

Afghanistan chews them up
like a giant paper shredder
They look so young.

Boys and girls dressed
in crisp camouflage as if
going to a costume party.

They stand in line for
their last Starbuck latte
awaiting the plane
that will soon deploy them.

Some didn't finish school.
Some couldn't get a job.
Some are seeking adventure.

They leave behind
their innocence and their lives
will never be the same,
if they return.

Carolyn Locke
Troy, ME

Day After Day

for Lucy

Good mornin,' Luce. . . good night, Luce. . . for all
the hours of the day and all the days in the week and
all the weeks in the month and all the months in the year
and all the years, oh all the years, of your constant
presence, like the keel of a boat keeping this place
steady through all the comings and goings, *please
rise for a moment of silence,* a moment of remembrance
in which deep laughter bubbles up beside your beloved
brusqueness, the dichotomy of you, which delights
and puzzles, *rise for a moment of silence,*
for the fierceness of your love, for you, repository
of names, faces, and stories that breathed life into this
school, which is, after all, much more than a school,
a moment of silence for all the games and graduations,
births and deaths, accidents and illnesses you witnessed,
for the joy and comfort and yes, even the scowls you
offered, as wave after wave of students and colleagues
passed under your watchful eye, *a moment of silence,*
Luce, is not enough, but day after day, steady as your
own presence, *we will rise and think of you. . .*
good mornin,' Luce. . . good night, Luce. . .

F. Anthony D'Alessandro
Celebration, FL

Arc Angel

Vacationing in Paris, my wife Adele and I asked our friends and fellow travelers to join us on a visit to the *Arc De Triumph*. Paris without that side trip, and a tour of the *Arc de Triumph* would have seemed like a visit to the Metropolitan Opera House on a day that both instruments and musicians were absent. Initially, however, we decided to stroll toward the Eiffel Tower. While squatting in its muscular shadow, we explored its magnificence. The meandering slow moving ribbon like lines knotted around the entry dampened our enthusiasm for exploring that monument.

Instead, we shared sips of *Merlot* wine, sat on its apron of grass, and snacked on some French bread. Minutes later, we ambled toward the *Arc de Triumph*. Our friends Peter and Athena assured us that an elevator delivered a smooth ride to the top of that monument. The day before, while crossing a narrow footbridge, Athena refused to take another step to traverse that shivering and shaky, one story bridge. Peter gently coaxed the sweating, crimson faced woman to backtrack off the structure. Only a day later, the couple seemed confident that Athena would handle the ride to the top of the *Arc* easily and without a trace of angst.

The *Arc de Triumph* line proved inviting. Only a few people stood before us by the ascending elevator. Peter and Athena felt confident and secure in the elevator because similar to an airplane, its closed in cabin seemed to shelter Athena from her fears.

The elevator stopped just below the roof. Forced to make a short stairway climb to the summit, we blocked Athena's view by encouraging her to walk near the wall. She managed to inch her way to the topside. At the *Arc de Triumph*'s summit, she clutched onto her hubby Peter's arm and gingerly explored the roof. Standing two arms lengths away from the

F. Anthony D'Alessandro
Celebration, FL

outside perimeter, with Peter's arms draped around her like an octopus its prey, she took photographs of the enchanting Parisian panorama. Her chin raised slightly, she freed herself, ventured toward the wall, and engaged in a sort of walking Braille, feeling, touching, and inching her way around.

Watching Athena's bravery, despite her fears and battle with terror, I offered to take her photos at the fence's edge with her camera. Politely, she declined my offer. Slowly and hesitantly she worked her way toward the outer perimeter and snapped photographs of *Sacre Coeur* Church, the Eiffel Tower, and the *Champs d'Elysseus*. Supported by her husband, she teetered from spot to spot and took the scenic shots she selected.

After a fifteen minute stay, my wife asked Athena to descend to street level. Athena immediately sped up, grabbed Adele's arm and demonstrated her readiness to return to the street. Before their leaving, I requested that after they reached the bottom, they look up and take our photos as Peter and I perched atop the *Arc*. "Just be on the lookout for our red shirts," I said.

Twenty minutes later, a pained Peter blurted behind a furrowed brow, "If we don't see the women in five minutes, I'm going down. They should have been there by now. I'm worried." I agreed. I heard an automobile backfire in the distance. That triggered me to pray to my guardian angel since I realized that Athena, was probably trembling by now. After Peter and I walked the entire rooftop, we looked down and saw the women waving and beckoning from the street. Relieved, we frenetically returned the gesture.

Once we realized that they'd taken our snapshots, we headed down. Failing to spot the elevator, I said, "Peter, I don't know how we could have missed that elevator." We continued walking down the stairs. When we reached the ground floor a fellow traveler suggested the down elevator had been reserved for emergencies and pregnant women.

We looked at each other and simultaneously mouthed,

F. Anthony D'Alessandro
Celebration, FL

"Athena!" Despite the fact that our wives waved a few moments ago, assured us of their safety, we scrambled to find them. Eventually, we met our spouses and they described what happened. About twenty steps into their descent, Athena staggered. They realized that the elevator was off limits to them. Adele, barely five feet tall failed to block Athena's view to the bottom. Clearly seeing the dizzying lower levels, Athena stood, then froze. They prayed. They prayed briefly. They prayed fervently. Adele said, "I heard a tiny explosive pop from below and immediately begged for my angel's help."

A wide-eyed Athena spoke, "Suddenly, from nowhere, he touched me. The man seemed as imposing as a college basketball player and stood about as tall as Peter. I looked twice at his gapped front teeth, just like my husband's, I noticed. His English sounded impeccable. Smiling broadly and reassuringly, he took my hand and gently tucked my arm under his. Then, he softly said, 'Let's go down, one step at a time.' As we descended, he chatted about the *Louvre*, about my love of art (don't know how he knew that), and the American expatriate writers of the Twenties. His voice sounded as powerful as Pavarotti's, yet comforting, like a mental massage." Surprisingly both Adele and Athena, usually suspicious of strangers, felt safe and secure in the man's presence.

Adele added, "That tortuous ten minute trip to the bottom passed so quickly." We both thanked him, he smiled, shook our hands and nodded affirmatively. A split second later we turned to offer a final word and he was gone. We looked all over, in every direction and he'd vanished. Athena added, "I don't know if he was an angel or not, but he arrived on the scene when we prayed and begged for help. He led us down gently and patiently."

Adele added, "He looked so much like Athena's Peter. Then, right after delivering us to safety, he just faded in the Parisian afternoon sun."

Robert B. Moreland
Pleasant Prairie, WI

Dog Days

A large turtle crosses
a tree shaded asphalt highway.
He defies death for a goal;
faith-born dreams he cannot see,
cool pond waits for him beyond.

A young squirrel stretches
full length down a bird feeder
reaching for a meal.
His eyes half-closed, seeds savored,
he's exposed in all his glory.

A midnight black grackle
plucks one yellow kernel
from under a lawn feeder.
With a triumphant squawk, he flies,
his golden eyes sparkling.

Eight tiny fluff balls
mother raccoon leads the way,
bandits' masks in place.
Feasting on old dog food
weaned at last, July begins.

Jennifer Reinard
Galena, OH

Human Kindness on Michigan Avenue

I remember your face;
you looked about seventy but
maybe time and circumstances were playing a trick on me
and you were younger than you seemed.

Deep blue eyes, weathered face, a grey beard dotted with
        crystallized
water vapor from your nose and mouth,
a tattered coat.
You kept your belongings close to you: a thin sheet with
        holes in it,
a bag of newspaper (your blankets?), and a cup.

You sat on the sidewalk, propped up against a building
at the southern end of the Magnificent Mile.
February—the wind sent daggers of cold off Lake Michigan
to pierce through our warm coats.

Three of us walked quickly along the avenue,
wrapped in the rapid, cozy fire of teenage self-absorption,
carrying on a conversation of little consequence and looking
forward to our day in the city, lunch in a hip restaurant,
paid for by our well-to-do grandmother who had sent us out
        on an adventure.

Businessmen and women hurried by, bracing against the
        cold in their haste to get
to meetings, pick up lunch, who knows what else.
They did not acknowledge your existence.
You were a fixture to them, like the planters in the middle of
the sidewalk containing summer's dead flowers,
or the *Do Not Walk* sign.

Jennifer Reinard
Galena, OH

We hurried past you and I looked down on you as we went
        by.
There, in your lap, rested an orange, incongruent against
        your rag-tag clothes and your bag of newspaper.
The orange was
                large, round, bright, perfect.
You looked at it, picked it up, fumbled with it, for your
        hands,
                red, raw, cracked, frozen
could not perform the task of removing the peel to get to the
        treasure
inside.

I stopped, mid-step, turned around into the sea of people
        bent against the wind
behind me, and
walked back to where you sat, propped up against the cold
        stone.

I removed my gloves—they were pink, green, yellow and blue,
        with flowers stitched on the top,
a gift from someone at Christmas.
I placed the gloves in your lap, near the orange, and shoved
        my hands into my
pockets.

Your eyes met mine, deep blue and surprised at the sudden
        arrival of the girl with
the gloves, and you said, *Thank you.*

I hope the orange tasted good.

Janet Morgan
Wiscasset, ME

Running Away

I was mad. I have no idea about what, but I was so mad that I decided to run away from home. I would go and live on my own. I hadn't a clue where I was going, but I would make everyone sorry for being mean to me. I would be gone and no one would be able to find me.

I don't need to answer to anyone else, I'd decided. *I'm old enough to be on my own.* I packed my small suitcase with one set of clothes, a few comic books, my favorite Hardy Boys mystery, and my guns. Taking care not to make any noise, I snuck downstairs. There I retrieved my toothbrush from the bathroom, clicked the suitcase shut, and closed the front door behind me for the last time.

I would walk to town. Or maybe someone would give me a ride. Then again, perhaps I would go to the Stickney farm. Less than a mile from my home—my former home, that is— I could hide out in their huge barn. After all, I was small for my age and I didn't take up much room. And I was sure no one would notice if I picked a few vegetables from their big garden out behind the barn. Besides, I had a friend inside the large, rambling farmhouse. Surely Diane would sneak me food from time to time.

Their big barn had a one-lane bowling alley on which we had frequently played imaginary games. I'm sure she would entertain me once more during my outings from one of the many rooms inside the barn. It was all coming together.

These options raced through my ten-year-old mind as I walked. And I had plenty of protection: I had my two cap guns and holster set. Maybe I would stop and put them on so people would realize I was not some hick kid out on her own. I watched western movies on television every Saturday morning and I knew how to take care of myself.

I slowed down as I proceeded away from my former home.

Janet Morgan
Wiscasset, ME

My feet dragged. I kicked up the dirt on the side of the road. Was it really so bad at home?

I thought about the good times: sitting on the living room floor opposite my mother, eating ice cream while we put together the jigsaw puzzle laid out on the coffee table, sharing a whole watermelon with the family while sitting around the kitchen table, swinging with my kid brother on the old tire my father had attached to a tall tree, running around the yard, playing cowboys and Indians with my cousin Dea.

I walked for what seemed to be hours before I decided to turn around. Well, maybe it had only been about 15 minutes, but it seemed as if I had left home hours ago. And no one had come looking for me!

I was on my way back home before I realized what I really wanted: to have my mother come running after me with distress etched on her face. I'd wanted her to beg me to come back. She would be sorry for being mean to me. But she hadn't come after me. Maybe she didn't even know I'd gone away. That would be the ultimate.

I made it all the way back home without a single neighbor raising the alert. Perhaps there was a posse out looking for me. Perhaps everyone had gone in the other direction on Birch Point Road. Yes, that was it. They thought I had gone to Dea's house. My mother was down there searching for me right now!

Well, I would just sneak back inside, unpack my bag, and see how long it took before they found me. The house was quiet. I made it back up to my room and put everything away, all but the toothbrush. I turned to take that back to the bathroom downstairs when I heard Eddie in the next room.

He always occupied the same smaller bedroom next to mine. I peeked into his room, where he was sitting on the floor playing with his Matchbox cars and trucks. Looking up, he asked, "What have you been doing? Reading?" Eddie knew how much I enjoyed books.

Janet Morgan
Wiscasset, ME

"Yup," I lied. I wondered why Eddie would be alone in the house. He, after all, had yet to turn six. Mom never left him alone. "Where's Mom?"

"Downstairs. She's making fudge." Eddie jumped up at the thought. "Let's go see if it's done yet."

I shoved the toothbrush into the back pocket of my jeans and followed my kid brother downstairs and into the kitchen. Sure enough, Mom had finished making the fudge and had started to bake a cake for tonight's dessert. She hadn't missed me at all! When she saw me, however, she told me that she was sorry she'd hurt my feelings and handed me a large piece of fudge.

As I took the fudge from my mother's outstretched hand, it occurred to me that she just might have known all along about my foray into strange territories. And then the sound of her voice interrupted my thoughts.

"And when you're finished, take that toothbrush from your back pocket and brush your teeth," Mom said with a knowing smile on her face. I hadn't fooled her at all. A warm feeling enveloped me—or maybe the taste of the best chocolate fudge in the world made me I realize that life had just become perfect again.

***

Patrick T. Randolph
Kalamazoo, MI

Soul Medication

Chickadee's

      Winter song—

           Patch of blue sky.

John T. Hagan
Springboro, OH

Bucolic Images

Yellow cat slumbers on stoop bench by screen door, dreaming of sparrows and mice.

Border Collie keeps somnolent vigil, snout between forepaws in shade of maple tree.

Quarter Horses swish tails while munching hay near water trough, salt block, and paddock fence.

Cicadas whine in trees, fulfilling each year's promise to repeat their cacophony in August-September.

Humming Birds keep frenetic pace, sucking nectar from daylilies that skirt slumping summer kitchen.

Sultry breezes tumble over leafy stalks, forming breakers on verdant lake of waving soybeans.

Alfalfa wafts from hayloft and saturates the air in horse stalls, alleyway, and tack room.

Dooryard tree drops apples, pocked by sorties flown by Yellow Jacket raiders.

Red-Tailed Hawk screeches retreat from woods and across lane, put to flight by squadron of militant crows.

Turkey Vultures, high in distance, circle languorously over carrion, for which they will soon come to table.

John T. Hagan
Springboro, OH

Dust Devils form and vanish in tractor run where banked sides yield to flat stretch near crop field.

Antebellum house creaks in ninety-degree heat, transforming second floor into farm-style sauna.

Woodpecker's tapping resonates from creek bed, as dogged digger excavates Sycamore.

Ancient Oak scatters acorns into rain grooves and tire ruts of graveled lane.

John Deere's tires send mournful rhythms from road, through trees, and over fields.

Manure piles dapple pasture where tufts of fescue escape the grazing of voracious equines.

Setting Sun lounges atop woodlot, casting late day shadows from board fence on to pasture.

Rising Moon stakes his claim as alpha orb, staging himself between sailing clouds.

Barn Swallows commence erratic flights in pursuit of twilight quarry.

Hoot Owls, perched in Sycamores, begin querulous discussions of aquiline issues.

Night Queen Nyx shrouds the farmland and activates her nocturnal world.

Seated on porch swing, I soak my senses with sights, sounds, and smells of late-summer day, knowing glorious autumn soon returns on carrousel of seasons.

Marilyn Fleming
Pewaukee, WI

Dry Years

sheeted windows—
her sage broom sweeps sweeps
—"a kerchiefed face"

black sunday—
a wall of rolling dust
squats in corners

devil winds
drifted over fencerows—
blistered hope

dry thunderstorms
sleeping in a dust bowl
—salty dreams

a dowsing rod—
the long legged rainmaker
sheds her skin

Published in *Cattails* premier edition
December 2013 United Haiku and Tanka Society

Goose River Anthology, 2014//18

Stephanie Guerin Batterman
Bath, ME

Helen's Storm

Helen lay in bed remembering the argument with her daughter. She had no idea how or why the arguments happened. She had never been able to figure it out. It seemed as if a great gulf lay between her and Jane, and she had no idea how to bridge it. She wasn't even sure how it had begun.

"Jane knows almost nothing about me," she thought. "It is my own fault really. How could I ever speak to my own daughter about my life? How could I speak to anyone about it?" And she never had. Her past lay like a hard lump in the middle of her chest, blocking her ability to connect with any-one.

"I feel this hardness," she thought. "It's like a rock. It is always there. It keeps me from speaking. The only way I can try to speak is through anger. I know this. Why can't I change it?" Tears began to flow; tears no one else had ever seen. She buried her face in her pillow so that her daughter would not hear. Jane slept in the little attic room right above her. It would be easy for her to hear her mother's weeping.

"Whatever would she think?" Helen asked herself. "What would she make of my crying? All she has ever seen is my anger. My tears would probably frighten her even more."

As she lay there crying softly, she felt the storm coming long before it arrived. She felt it in her bones and in her own heart. The texture of the air changed and was charged with something sinister, evil. It frightened her, even more than her own thoughts did.

As the storm arrived, she heard Jane's footsteps on the floor above her head.

"I hope she is not coming to check on me," Helen thought. She knew that sometimes Jane opened her bed-

Stephanie Guerin Batterman
Bath, ME

room door in the dark of night. She had heard the soft open-
ing of her door and felt Jane's quiet presence there. Helen
never moved on those occasions. She pretended to be in a
deep sleep. She would not have known what to say to her
daughter. She never knew why Jane came to her room. Did
she need something? Was she worried about her mother?
Did she simply stand there quietly hating her mother? Helen
had never dared to ask.

But Jane's steps stopped and Helen thought she was
probably standing at her little window watching the storm.

The storm sounded fierce to Helen and she was afraid.
So she did what she always did when she was alone in her
room and frightened. She crept softly from her bed. It was
quite dark in her room, but the light cast by the nightlight
she kept there, gave enough light for her to move safely.
Moving as quietly as she could, she got the small stool that
sat beside her closet, opened the closet door, placed the stool
in front of the clothes rod and stepped up. She reached back
as far as she could and touched the old hatbox that was hid-
den there. It had been her mother's sewing box many years
ago. It had been a beautiful cream-colored box with bright
pink roses printed on it back then. Now it was browning with
age and the roses had faded to a dull tan, but she had kept
it as the only reminder of her mother.

Clutching it to her chest, she stepped down and tip-toed
back to her bed. She placed the box next to her and opened
it carefully. Rolled inside was the familiar patchwork blan-
ket she had made so many years ago. No one else had ever
seen it. It was her secret, her most precious possession.

When her husband Joe had left, she had secretly taken
all his old worn plaid flannel shirts and cut them into
squares. These she had stitched together into the blanket
she now held in her hands. As always she immediately
raised it to her face and breathed in the familiar scent that
always calmed her. Yes, she had loved him. No one would
ever have guessed how much. She knew she had driven him

Stephanie Guerin Batterman
Bath, ME

away with her suspicions and accusations. It made her ill to think of how she had treated him. She could never have explained her fears to him. She hardly knew their source herself. All she knew was that his love for their child had sent chills of fear through her like a knife. Whenever Joe had played with Jane, taking her on his knee and playing his fingers along Jane's cheek, a shiver of cold blackness enveloped her and she could not help but scream at him.

She knew how bewildered he had been. He had begged her to explain. He had wanted so much to understand, to calm her, to let her know that everything was all right. But she could not voice her fears to him, to anyone. So, in the end, Joe had left. All she had of him now was this treasured blanket, this secret that she held to herself like a child holds a beloved toy. It was all she had left of the love she had once known.

She could hear the storm raging outside. She did not hear any footsteps from above, so she assumed that Jane was still standing in the cold watching the storm. Helen felt safe from discovery.

Clutching the soft quilt to her chest, she got back under the covers. It was cold in her room. She knew it was freezing outside in the storm, and she shivered from the coldness and the extra chill that seemed to come from her very soul.

"I wonder," she thought. "I wonder if I still have a soul or was that what was stolen from me so very long ago?" Harshly, she tried to push the thought from her mind. "Not now!" her mind screamed. "Not now! Not ever!" But the storm outside had entered her heart and she could no longer hold back the memories.

She saw herself then as a little brown-haired seven year-old, with short bangs and long pigtails that had bright red ribbon bows tied at the ends. The pigtails were flying out behind her as she ran to catch up with her brother.

"Wait! Wait for me!" she called as she ran, but he was ahead of her. He was running home because he had seen

Stephanie Guerin Batterman
Bath, ME

their uncle's familiar car pull up in front of their house. It was always a great treat when Uncle Eric came to visit.

Uncle was standing near the back of his car and had a big grin on his face. This was a good sign as it meant that he had brought treats for them which he always kept in his car trunk. As her brother arrived at his car, he was greeted by one of Uncle's big bear hugs. Helen arrived just in time to squeeze into that hug. Both she and her brother looked with anticipation at Uncle's car, and Uncle Eric laughed that big booming laugh of his and opened the trunk with a flourish. There lay a bag of licorice for her brother and a small turtle in a little bowl for her.

Helen squealed with delight and took the bowl carefully from the car. "I'll name him Willy," she said, "after Dad."

Uncle pulled his suitcase from the car, and they followed him into the house.

"Look, Mom, look who's here! It's Uncle Eric, and he's going to stay a while."

Helen knew this because of the suitcase. Uncle didn't always bring his things with him, so the suitcase was a clue that he was staying.

Mom greeted Eric, who was actually her uncle, making him Helen's great-uncle, but Helen could never get all that stuff straight in her head, so she just called him Uncle.

The afternoon flew by with great merriment as Uncle always had great tales to tell of his adventures on the open road. That's what he always called his stories, "Tales of the Open Road." Each time he came he had new and more outrageous tales to tell. She, being the youngest, always got the privilege of sitting on his lap as he spoke. This day she held in her lap Willy in his little bowl. There was no doubt in Helen's mind that Uncle Eric was her favorite person in the whole wide world.

"Stop now!" Helen's mind cried as she lay in her bed holding the flannel quilt to her chest. "Please let the memories stop here. I was happy then. It was probably this last

Stephanie Guerin Batterman
Bath, ME

moment in my life that I was truly happy."

But it was too late. The memories she had suppressed for so long had taken on a life of their own. It seemed as if they had joined the raging of the storm outside her window and there was no way to stop them.

She saw herself in her long nightgown getting ready to get into her bed.

"Uncle Eric," she called, "can you tell me one more story? Please," she begged.

She heard his footsteps on the stairs, one step at a time, she heard them. She scrambled into bed, turned out her light, and waited. She saw him then. He was a dark outline standing in the doorway with the hall light behind him. He seemed to stand there a long time and she held her breath wondering if he had changed his mind. Finally he came into the room, but instead of sitting at the end of her bed as he usually did, he came to the side of her bed and kneeled on the floor next to her.

"Quiet, now," he said softly. "Just be still."

He began to touch her gently, first her face and then her arms and hands. It felt strange, but good in a way. Then he reached under the covers and began to touch her all over. He lifted her nightgown and continued to touch her.

Her body became very still as if that would stop his hands. Her mind screamed, but no sound came out of her mouth. She did not know what was happening but she knew it was all wrong—all wrong! Her mind flew up and away from what was happening to her. She lay perfectly still, but she was no longer really there. She was somewhere else, far away. She was not in that room and what was happening there was not happening to her.

She had never said anything about that night. She never spoke of Uncle Eric again. When he visited after that, she did not greet him, did not listen to his stories, and never went to bed until he left. If he stayed overnight, she hid in her closet until she knew he was asleep on the couch downstairs.

Stephanie Guerin Batterman
Bath, ME

She gave her turtle "Willy" to her brother, who told her later that he had taken it to the frog pond and let it go. She had been happy about that because she never wanted to see it again. It would remind her. She hadn't wanted anything to remind her.

Helen heaved a great sigh and sobbed into the warm quilt. "That was it," her mind screamed. "That was the moment my whole life changed."

She became known as a serious child, a quiet child. She did well in school and was helpful and obedient at home. Inside she carried the terrible secret—the knowledge that there was something very wrong with her. She worked hard to bury this knowledge, afraid that if she were too aware of it, it would somehow leak out and others would know.

This strategy worked well for many years. When she met Joe, she fell instantly and deeply in love with him. He was so kind to her—so gentle—that she was able to forget Uncle Eric and that terrible night. But when their daughter was born and Joe had told her stories and played with her, the darkness would come over her—the darkness that had covered her memories for all the years, and she would scream in distress. The memories would begin to appear and the only way to stop them, was to scream, accuse, suspect. Not even she understood what was happening at the time. She did not want to understand; she just wanted it to stop. She wanted anything that reminded her of that night to stop.

Helen realized then that this secret was the barrier between herself and her own daughter. It had been the thing that had driven Joe away from her.

The storm in her heart seemed to match the storm outside. She lay there, clinging to her beloved quilt and sobbing quietly. She knew when the storm ceased for she heard Jane's gentle footsteps as she returned to her bed upstairs.

All was quiet now, except for her heart. These memories had been buried for such a long time. She hated that they had returned with such power, and wondered how she would go on from here. Could she bury them again? Would they haunt her even more now that they were so close to the surface of her mind?

She meant to put her quilt back in its secret place, but she was exhausted from her inner turmoil. So she stayed in her bed, her mind in chaos, her heart nearly broken.

She did not know that she had finally slept until she was startled awake by Jane's footsteps on the stairs. The memories of the night came flooding back to her and she was afraid again. She had no idea how to go on. She did not even want to get out of bed—ever.

When she heard Jane rattling dishes in the kitchen, she became aware that she still had the quilt in her hands, held tightly against her body. This frightened her into action. She knew that sometimes, after she and Jane had had an argument, Jane would bring a cup of tea to her room. Helen supposed this was Jane's way of apologizing, but they never spoke about their arguments at those times. Jane would simply hand her the cup of tea and walk to Helen's window and open the curtains. She might ask Helen about her plans for the day or tell her when she might be home from work. But then she would go back downstairs, leaving Helen with her tea and her thoughts.

She jumped from her bed and quickly rolled the quilt into a ball and placed it back into the old hatbox. She got the stool from its place by the closet door, hoping to get the box safely hidden before Jane arrived with tea. She heard Jane's steps on the stairs and knew she had to hurry. Quickly, she stepped up, but her foot landed at the edge of the stool and toppled over sending Helen crashing to the floor. The box fell beside her and flew open, spilling the quilt on the floor beside her.

Jane rushed into the room and ran to her mother dropping the tea cup as she ran..

"Are you all right?" she cried. "Are you hurt?"

"I think I am okay," Helen responded. "Help me up."

Stephanie Guerin Batterman
Bath, ME

As Jane reached down to help her mother, she noticed the old hatbox and the quilt spread out beside it.

"What were you doing?" Jane asked. "And what is that? I've never seen it before, but somehow it is familiar."

Helen began to cry then. Instead of lifting her mother, Jane dropped to the floor beside her. Helen fell into Jane's arms with great heaving sobs. Jane was surprised by this, shocked even. She could not remember ever being this close to her mother. She could not remember ever holding her or being held by her. Jane was so stunned that she simply sat there, holding her mother and wondering what was happening.

They sat there for a long time, mother and daughter together. To both of them, in different ways, it felt a bit like last night. The room felt just like the world had felt before the storm arrived, as if the air itself was charged with anticipation, but anticipation of what neither mother nor daughter knew clearly.

Jane could not help herself. The questions came pouring out before she could think, before she could stop them. "What is it, Mother? What's wrong? What were you doing? How did you fall? What is that quilt? Why have I never seen it before?"

Somewhere, deep inside her sobs, Helen thought, "Now it is done. My secret is out. Now I will have to tell her everything."

With tears in her eyes, Helen looked up at Jane. "I love you," she whispered. "I have always loved you."

Stunned, Jane held her mother more tightly and said, "It will be okay, Ma. It will all be okay."

Sally Belenardo
Branford, CT

Morning After Rain

Near brook and pond she listens;
the sounds of rain have ceased.
There is work to do before
the Earth spins farther east.

She dons a gown of sunbeams
and lays aside her cloak,
pulls up her misty stockings
as vapor lifts like smoke.

She stretches on a meadow
and combs her flaxen hair,
leaving strands of diamonds
for grass and twigs to wear.

She takes the stars she gathered
while clouds obscured the skies,
and drops them on drenched hemlocks,
to sparkle, though night dies,

then wakes the drowsy thicket
and shines the rising stream,
polishes the river stones
and makes the cobwebs gleam.

With nimble, golden fingers
she sets a songbird free;
joyously he praises her,
high in a glistening tree.

Sylvia Little-Sweat
Wingate, NC

After Reading Nikki Giovanni

I am not black, but I am more than Southern
white. As a Forties' child I hugged black Mary
on our white share-cropping farm. As a Fifties'-
Sixties' teen when all things seemed in-between
I heard whites disclaim integration and felt
ashamed. I dreamed the dream of Martin Luther
King and Rosa Parks. As a Seventies—On career
woman, I embraced all students black or white—
most especially those with I'll-Kick-Your-Ass
attitudes—as I tried, win or lose, to teach the blues
of being more or less than a certain hue. As an
Eighties' wife I learned endurance, the black art
of somehow holding a family together when it
shattered like a white porcelain bowl. And as I
mothered my more-than-white Southern mother
at the nursing home, I watched black women make
Mother's care a way of loving me as well. So . . .
in a South still often seen as black and white, I must
state that I fail to see any innate cleft in humanity.
All hearts beat just human beats, are neither black
nor white, but only red—only red—when truly read.

Craig Merrow
Wells, ME

Ice Cream

Davy, Pat, Karen and Joshua were sitting around the kitchen table one summer evening making ice cream when the phone rang, interrupting the serenity of the gentle hum of the fan spinning lazily overhead. Davy reached up behind him to answer it while everyone else carried on with their conversation.

"This sure is good!" exclaimed Pat as she popped another spoonful into her mouth.

"I'll say!" added Karen.

Joshua swallowed his mouthful and replied, "Homemade ice cream is hard to beat on a hot night like this."

"What? Really?" said Davy into the phone.

"It was a lot of work," said Karen, "but it sure was worth it."

"Gotta love those old-fashioned kitchen utensils," said Pat. "I never even knew they used to make it like this. It's very satisfying to do it yourself."

Joshua nodded. "Davy's mom has all kinds of neat stuff like that..."

"Swahili!" exclaimed Davy.

Joshua gave Davy a puzzled glance, then continued, "It was a lot of fun to make it that way."

"Swahili!" repeated Davy.

Karen ignored Davy as she replied, "You know, sometimes I think we have it too easy; we've become overly dependent on technologies that we don't always need."

"Or can't afford," added Pat. "It's ridiculous what they charge for some things."

"No? How about Mandarin?" asked Davy.

"Dad was telling me that everyone used to get along fine without all these electronic gadgets; now people wonder what they would ever do without them." said Joshua. "It's kind of

Craig Merrow
Wells, ME

ironic how technology brings us closer together, but isolates us from each other at the same time. People don't always take the time to appreciate the simple things in life."

Pat gestured into her bowl with her spoon. "Like the antique ice cream maker; it was more work, but the results were worth the effort."

"It's all about instant gratification these days," noted Karen as she scooped more ice cream into her bowl. "Nobody wants to wait for anything."

"I didn't ask for Spanish," scolded Davy. "How about Tonga?"

Joshua glanced at Davy before saying, "Sometimes the anticipation of something is more fun than the object you are pursuing."

"Not even Makhuwa? No? Okay, good-bye," sighed Davy as he hung up the phone before digging into his ice cream.

There was a long pause before Pat finally asked, "Do we want to know what that was all about?"

Davy looked up from his bowl. "What? Oh, that," he replied. "It was some telemarketer call, and the first question they asked me is what language I wanted to converse in."

"But you don't speak any of those languages," noted Joshua.

"Neither did they," shrugged Davy. "Let's make some more ice cream!"

Lorelee L. Sienkowski
Packwaukee, WI

The Samaritan Woman

Always a "server," she went at mid-day
To gather fresh water required to pray.
To add to confusion
A Jew blocked her way
By claiming the ground
Where she needed to lay.

The well was a dug one:
A hole in the ground.
The water was deep
But cold and quite sound.

"I'm thirsty," the man said.
"Please bring me a drink."
She bristled inside her,
How dare he to think
That she was to serve him,
This Jew at the brink.

"You haven't a bucket—
You're Jewish, I'm not—
We shouldn't be speaking—
I'm sorry you're hot."

"I know that you've married,
Five times in the past,
Just not to this new one,
Another outcast.
But I've brought you water
That will ever last."

Lorelee L. Sienkowski
Packwaukee, WI

"You know so much of me,
Although we've just met,
You must be a prophet;
Come stay and we'll fete.
"I'm more than a prophet,"
The Savior did say,
"I am the Messiah,
Please hear what I say."

She gathered her neighbors,
They sat all around
To hear the Messiah
With news so profound.

I'm thirsty, Messiah,
Please bring me a drink—
Your Life-Giving water
My needs quickly shrink.

***

Forsaken

Having finished their chores decorating
the altar, Reception, or deck,
like chickens and bunnies in springtime,
poinsettias sit abandoned in back
Recovery always takes loving:
we gather some into our room,
show patience and water and caring
'til next winter's light brings back bloom.

Elmae Passineau
Wausau, WI

The Ones That Got Away

A gang of old men
this brisk January morning
warm their thick blue-veined hands
around sturdy white mugs
The dark bitter coffee—
or maybe tan and sweet—
steaming comfort for gnarled fingers
that once wielded hammers or shovels,
winches or wrenches

A cluster of navy windbreakers fading to gray
and cracked leather jackets worn to softness
drape the hump-backed chairs
Once, there would have been a pungent blue cloud
overhead and a tray heaped with ashes,
but that's gone, too, along with lush hair,
tight stomachs, and strong knees

They eye new patrons as they come
through the door, almost proprietarily,
almost intimidating them,
but they're only looking for familiar faces
for their diminished crew
They refill their mugs
and talk of old war buddies, fishing trips,
and perhaps beautiful women they have known.
All the ones that got away.

Edie Schmoll
Menifee, CA

Something New!

Don't write me a poem
of the birds and the bees.
Enough already!
so Something New, please.

And don't start again
on the sunsets and flowers.
There's enough out there now
killing too many hours.

I don't want an epic
on rainbows or brooks.
Let's hear it, instead,
about people, or books.

Or maybe on music,
or art—NOT the view.
Do you think it would kill you
to pen Something New?

So don't ramble on
about nature and dawn.
Give me grief, give me glory—
but TELL ME A STORY!

Jean M. B. Lawrence
Waldoboro, ME

Sedony's Story

At age eighty-five, Sedony Welt managed her knitting needles without a glance as she turned the heel on a woolen sock while recounting for her great grandchildren, who visited often and sat about her chair, the stories of the deer and fox that lived nearby. On her better days, she could still stir up a batter and fry donuts or bake a pot of beans in her daughter-in-law's kitchen. Her dress and shawl were neat and clean, and she kept her hair pulled back into a soft bun at the nape of her neck. Folks in the Wagner Bridge neighborhood of 1841 considered her a handsome woman, a fine example of graceful aging.

But, as the sun colored the western expanse of her home's acreage, she would readily admit the late afternoon was a favorite time. The moments she spent alone in her rocking chair, when the sunbeams warmed her shawl and most of the activity of the house centered in the kitchen, belonged to her alone. Her knitting and sewing laid aside, her daily meditations completed, she was able to rest, relax and delve into her memories: her memories of Blasius, their youth and their dreams. And today, her mind traveled back over fifty years to that day of decision when, with Blasius listening, she had wrestled with a momentous decision.

***

The March wind whipped Sedony's cape as she walked the path which led up the hill and through the woods. Her steps were deliberate and the pace steady. Her babe, tucked tightly within her shawl, slept soundly, safe and warm next to her body. In her right hand, she held three pussy willow branches, early signs of the spring to come, brought to her this morning by Charles, John and Elizabeth. The children

Jean M. B. Lawrence
Waldoboro, ME

had rejoiced in finally being allowed outdoors after the three day storm that had drenched the fields and streams which fed the Medomak River that bordered the farm. Their elder sister Susannah had taken them to the marsh where they found the willow branch offerings.

While the rain had ceased, it would take several days before the fields dried up, and Sedony could feel the spongy ground sink under her feet as she moved into the woods on her way to the Schuman burial yard. In the distance, the stones, some beginning to show signs of accumulating lichens and mosses, came into sight, but her gaze fastened on the obviously new gravesite in the upper left corner. Her words of last fall came to mind; she had spoken them to Old Man Schuman when after the woods accident, he had offered a place in his family's yard for Blasius' body, "Please put him as close to his home as possible." And so, a grave had been dug close to the line which marked the boundary.

Picking up a branch here or twigs there as she moved among the sparsely placed stones, she automatically made her way to her love's final resting place. She sank to her knees oblivious of the wet ground, brushed away an acorn and pine tassels, and deliberately laid the willow branches before the single field stone which marked the head of Blasius' bed. Then the refrain that she had spoken when first she made her way alone to this site came back clearly:

"Why, Blasius, why? Just when we were growing our farm and family, just when we had established the foundation for our dream, why did you have to leave? The children miss you so much. Each dusk, I find them listening for the tread of your boots at the back door, waiting for your call reminding them of our shared supper, and your hugs and rough bearded kisses. I listen to hear you question the boys about their chores or compliment Susanna on her jelly roll cake. I find myself searching for the twinkle in your blue eyes promising future moments of shared joys between us. You are so sorely missed by your family."

Jean M. B. Lawrence
Waldoboro, ME

Often she had poured out such words in those conversations of those early fall days. She had recited promises that she hoped would assure him that she would create a secure future for their family.

The Newbert brothers had assured her that they would continue to work the wood lot and that her share of the profit would provide for the basics needed by her family. Her parents were close by and would help with the upbringing of the children. Despite his removal to this eternal bed, the dream for which Blasius had left his German homeland, hired on with the British as a paid mercenary, and walked miles from Fort George at Castine to Waldoboro to earn enough money to purchase land of his own burned brightly in her heart during those fall visits. It was a dream of a land inheritance for his sons, something he had never known. It had sustained him for close to forty years and was one that she had adopted as her own when they married fourteen years ago.

But today, Sedony, though once more on her knees, had no words of hope, for her world was crashing down about her. A week after Blasius' death, word came from the representatives of General Knox that the claims of 101 inhabitants of lands along the east side of the Medomak River were determined by them to be invalid. Hers was among them. The fact that Blasius and Sedony had purchased their acreage in good faith from John and Lucy Martin seven years ago, had worked and improved the holding made no difference to General Knox. In fact, it was to his benefit, for the improvements had increased the value of the property. Legally, Knox had gained the rights to the Waldo heirs' original grant holdings, purchased others, and now wanted to create a personal fiefdom with the contended farms. His plan was as grandiose as his physical size; he reveled in promised power and lifestyle as a landlord with numerous tenants at his fingertips: all to be provided by the Waldo grant. Knox's lawyers were pressing his case with zeal.

Jean M. B. Lawrence
Waldoboro, ME

Sedony had no cash with which to repurchase her acres, even though Knox's lawyers assured her that the plan he offered was more than fair. Along with the other landholders in the same situation, only one pathway was before them: band together with the blessings and support of the fledgling town and fight the action in court with no real promise that they could or would win. No one knew how long the fight might take, and from the actions of the court in Boston, few were interested in fighting a hero of the Revolution who had chosen to retire to his wife's inherited holdings.

"Blasius, you taught me to love our land and the river. You gave me your dream to share. Our bed, fashioned by your own hands from wood you cut on our land, where we shared the joys and passion of our life together, where I birthed three of our children with only you to help me, where I washed your body before consigning you to this plot, is empty and cold. No longer is it an active symbol of our promises and dreams; no longer does it provide warmth and comfort. My life, like our bed, is cold and lonely without you. Please, Blasius, help my unbelief, tell me what to do, where to turn. Give me a sign. Before me, I see only one sure form of relief from this pain of loss."

Sweeping the grave with a pine branch, Sedony rose, gave one quick glance and whispered, "'Til later, love."

She moved away quickly, not along her original path but on a second trail which led to the river and a site overlooking the turbulent waters, a spot to which her lover had taken her when first he proposed marriage, a hidden haven they had shared with no one else throughout their fourteen years of marriage.

Just over the rise, Sedony could hear Charles and John arguing about their daily chore of gathering kindling. She put their voices out of her mind as she sat, leaned over the rocky ledge, and stared down into the whirlpool that today was vigorously churning. This was not an unfamiliar place and sight; in fact it was one to which she had often come for

Jean M. B. Lawrence
Waldoboro, ME

respite over the years. The pool was always deep and moving; nothing thrown into it stayed on its surface, for the river was alive here and seemed to gobble up all that came its way. Whether alone or accompanied by Blasius, her soul was always nourished by the beauty and power that nature through the river revealed in this place. Hope was rekindled, no matter what the problem or joy.

One step was all it would take to end forever the pressure that seemed to be smothering the life from her body. One step and she would be safe, once again, in the arms of Blasius. The children, with Susanna to lead them, would go to her parents' home. They would be safe, loved and cared for just as she had been. The babe who hardly ever left her side, her last gift from her love, would easily travel downward with her. She had thought over this action for the days since the lawyers had appeared at her door pressing Knox's demand. No longer would loneliness eat at her existence. No longer would the worry about planning, planting, harvesting and cutting wood, exercises that her husband had easily carried on his shoulders, be problems for her to solve.

"It will end," she said aloud as she stood and stepped toward the ledge's edge. As she moved, John's voice rang out,

"Mother! Mother!"

Quickly she turned towards his voice, and the baby stirred. She felt her milk descend as Mathias in his infant way rooted for her breast seeking sustenance and the comfort of his mother.

***

He stood tall and straight in the doorway to Sedony's room. Hoping to gently awaken her for the family's evening meal, he spoke, "Mother, Mother."

When she didn't respond to his soft call, Mathias entered the room and knelt at Sedony's side. As he placed his hand on her shoulder, he realized that she had stepped from this

Jean M. B. Lawrence
Waldoboro, ME

world into the next. She was gone and with her the comfort that she had always provided her family.

***

Afterward: Sedonia Welt, along with 30 other residents of the town who lived along the river, fought in the courts for ten years to keep her land and lost. In 1803, she paid a second time for hers and Blasius' 200 acres: $176 plus interest, a bargain by our standards, a fair price by the standards of the court of her day.

***

Ann M. Penton
Green Valley, AZ

Ivan's Impact
In response to Hurricane Ivan

pods of grey dolphins
caught in Ivan's spin cycle—
what about breathing?

atop wide-flung sand
dashes of fish floundering—
battered shorebirds feast

sand dollars gobbled—
Hurricane Ivan spits up
nothing but small change

Hannah Fox Trowbridge
Harpswell, ME

You're Welcome

Whatever happened
to the two words, "You're Welcome!"
Rarely uttered now.

***

Liz Moser
Baltimore, MD

Israeli Arab

The land is an anomaly,
pressing past to present,
touching us with dust and smell
and noises other ages knew.
Remnants of Crusaders' bloody swords
and Moslem scimitars
are buried next to guns held tight
by Holocaust survivors who deny
the land a common ownership.
Dung and dirt and chained dog's howl
are backdrop to the Arab man who talks to us—
his words deny the squalor
and his people's degradation.
He speaks of hope and peace and progress
pouring coffee into plastic cups—
how can we drink his dark, sweet coffee in this bitter dust?
How can we not?

Sylvia Little-Sweat
Wingate, NC

Lilacs

A little girl's nose
nudges lavender petals
and scatters the bees.

Married just months before, the young woman digs a
> *flowerbed*
beside the porch. She pauses to rest her hands on the hoe
> *handle*
and to let the autumn sun dry her neck and face. Across
> *the fields*
a hawk circles high over the tree line. She is planting lilacs.

A puppy chases his shadow,
and bees, beside the lilacs.

The wind will whip around the north side of the house in
> *winter*
and down the porch, she reasons. This is the right place
> *for lilacs,*
to face them south. Breezes can still feel cold when new
> *spring green*
matches the lilacs' heart-shaped leaves.

When do hearts know
that lilacs follow snow?

Sylvia Little-Sweat
Wingate, NC

A mother now, she stands at the porch's edge. Her baby's
        breath
in the hollow of her neck is softer than the April air. The
        work
of giving birth weakened her, so she leans her hip against
        the brick
column. Underneath his tiny wrist, the veins are the color of
        lilacs.

In time her son, too,
chooses the corner of the porch
when lilacs bloom.

She sits in the porch swing while her granddaughter
        unbraids
and combs her thin gray hair. Long shadows stretch from
        the woods
into the fields. Like old sachets of lavender in her bureau
        drawers,
the lilacs, too, hold the musk of many evenings.

Early evening,
even the deepest shadows
are edged in lilac.

Belva Ann Prycel
Alna, ME

The Call

There is an undertow in me
A deep unfettered pulsing tone;
That speaks of wave and sand and sea,
And breaks upon a shore alone.

A call within the lingering breath,
Of salt airs carried in the night;
That gather in my deep unrest,
On shores of youth, far from my sight.

So longingly I close my eyes,
See seagrass windrows on the shoals;
And iridescent shells that bide
In crystal-shining tidepool bowls.

I feel the secrets long concealed,
In wave-washed timbers, tossed and hewn,
Like weathered bones, their souls revealed
In racklines, drying, lost and strewn.

Or dunes replete with sumptuous fare,
Of bayberry and tangled vines;
On scalloped silver sands that bear
The winds in cryptic rippled lines.

My torn allegiance to the earth,
Is ever weak and frail in me;
A murmuring has called since birth,
The lonely heartbeat of the sea.

Nancy Freund Bills
South Portland, ME

Judith Or a Dish Served Cold

Judith Hertzog has set a small Italian dictionary on top of the white tablecloth; she's hoping to get by without using it. Like many American visitors, her Italian is limited. A waiter at Ristorante Sorrento attempts to get her attention, "Signora?"

Judith wipes her lips with a cloth napkin and examines the waiter's nametag. "Si, Gino."

"So you like your risotto?" Gino is teasing.

Judith has been eating the mushroom risotto with a gusto she hasn't experienced in years. The texture of the rice is grainy and creamy at the same time and the chunks of mushroom are meaty and fresh. Her appetite surprises her; it must be because she is going to kill Riccio today, November 7, 1999.

"The risotto is wonderful," Judith says. "Delicioso. Molto Bene. My compliments to the chef."

"So the Insalata Caprese now?" Gino asks. "Nothing else?"

"Gino, I'm old," Judith says. "I don't eat much."

"You're not so old. You're still 'elegante.' "

Judith has aged well, probably all the tennis and swimming. She was athletic and tall—five feet, nine inches. But now, she is not so athletic or so tall. After Judith received confirmation from her private investigator, Patrick O'Hara, that Riccio would be at the Ristorante Sorrento, she dressed carefully. She is wearing a Donna Karan dress, a travel knit in charcoal grey, and a silver necklace. Her thick grey and silver hair is shoulder length, and extra mascara accentuates the intensity of her grey eyes.

In two months, in January of 2000, Judith will be eighty. At her home in Boston, on the top of her desk, there is a plane ticket to Paris, an early birthday gift from her son-in-

Nancy Freund Bills
South Portland, ME

law, Benjamin Goldman.   Benjamin loved her daughter, Ruth, and was a devoted father to her granddaughter, Naomi. Both were killed by a hit and run driver in '75.

As a secular Jew, Judith holds few traditional beliefs, but she does believe that one's immortality is tied to the lives of one's children and grandchildren. When her only child and only grandchild were killed, she was devastated. The role that remains for her is to be a tool of Hebrew vengeance.

"Signora?" Gino waits until he has Judith's attention. "You like the Gavi? Another glass?"

"Si, grazie," Judith says. She turns to the restaurant's entrance when she hears the owner of the Ristorante Sorrento greet Dominic Riccio. Riccio is an older version of the drunken twenty-one year old who plowed his car into a group of fifth graders, their teachers, and their parent chaperones who were walking on a crosswalk on their way home from an outing to Sturbridge Village.

Judith reaches down to touch the straw purse on her lap. She reaches inside to feel the steely surface of her father's Python Colt revolver. Behave normally, she tells herself. Riccio is walking toward her, then past her to a table nearby. His face is fuller, his hairline has receded, he has a paunch, but otherwise, he is easy to identify. Twenty-five years, but he looks much like he did at his arraignment when he pled "not guilty" and his lawyer got him bail. Days later, *The Boston Globe* headlines screamed, HIT AND RUN DRIVER SKIPS BAIL. The police tracked Riccio to Chicago, to Las Vegas, to Miami, but then the trail went cold. Riccio has been missing until last month when O'Hara discovered him living in Sorrento.

Judith is worried. Riccio isn't alone. A thin, pale woman is sitting next to him and next to her is a girl of ten or eleven. Judith hasn't imagined this scenario. She can't shoot Riccio in front of a child.

"Signora, your wine." Gino fills Judith's glass, then follows her gaze. He makes a gesture of dismissal and "sotto

Nancy Freund Bills
South Portland, ME

voce," he mutters a phrase in Italian referring to Riccio as "American trash!" Judith holds her breath. But then, like a miracle, the woman and the girl stand and leave Riccio's table. Judith takes a small sip of the Gavi; she tastes its crisp finish.

The risotto has given Judith some needed energy and the wine, some courage. Her strategy is to get in close and squeeze two bullets into Riccio's chest. Afterward, she'll try to get back to her room on the third floor of the Hotel Paulo. Judith stands holding her straw bag in front of the gun to conceal it. She releases the trigger guard as her father taught her years ago. She walks to Riccio's table. "Dominic Riccio?" she demands. He nods assent and stands with no hint of recognition. She steps forward aiming the Colt directly at his chest. Without hesitation, she shoots the gun twice.

Riccio staggers. As he falls to the floor, Judith throws a glass of red wine at him. "Drunken murderer! Killer of children!" she cries out. "For my Ruth, for my Naomi," she exclaims. She has become the embodiment of her Old Testament namesake, Judith. Her enemy, her Holofernes, is dead.

Judith weaves through a back alley to her hotel room where she pours a glass of water and retrieves a cache of pain and sleep medication. The pills are enough to kill a mule. On the balcony, she looks out onto a small, rear courtyard. When she sits heavily in a metal chair, she thinks, this is where I'm going to die. From far down the Corso Italia, Judith hears sirens. The abrasive sirens of Europe are chilling and evocative of WW II and the Holocaust; they build to a shattering volume as they near Judith's hotel. She takes a sip of water, then a gulp. She spreads out the pills on the metal table.

But then something unexpected happens. The sirens continue past Hotel Paulo, past Judith. They disappear down the Via Marina, a narrow, winding street, to the Gulf of Naples. Maybe, Judith thinks, O'Hara has been successful

Nancy Freund Bills
South Portland, ME

in bribing the local police. Or maybe they are just glad to see the last of the "American trash."

Maybe, Judith thinks, she can go to Paris for her birthday after all. She sips the water, puts the pills away.

***

Lyn Lifshin
Vienna, VA

Late October

comes fast. Red
in the maples
blossoms over
night. Crickets
and birds lose
their songs in the
iced air. Soon
what hangs on
won't. Blood
stains from the
torn fox and
the ravaged deer
blur in the rain.
Open the last jar
of maple syrup
for any trace of
sweetness, light

Barbara J. Dorner
DePere, WI

Christmas Snow

On the night that Christ was born the angels watched from
     Heaven High,
But when they saw His precious face those angels all began
     to cry,
They clapped their hands, they flapped their wings,
They caused joyful Christmas breeze,
That turned the air around them cold and caused those
     angels' tears to freeze,
So teardrops fell to Earth from Heaven on that good and
     holy night,
Like pearls of frosting in the treetops, turning hills and
     valleys white,
Bestowing flakes of jubilation on God's creatures down
     below,
Filling hearts with fascination, and the Earth with
     Christmas Snow!

***

He Reached Out His Hands

Out popped my head, so I opened my eyes,
I was helpless and small, just an infant in size,
My own mother asleep with her cheek at my nose,
My poor father in shock counting fingers and toes,
So I stretched and I cooed, like a nestling dove,
When I heard the Lord's voice, it was sweetness and love!
He said "Welcome dear soul, I am Jesus, I Am,
And today is your birthday my sweet little lamb."
Then He laughed, and I smiled, and my tiny toes curled,
As he reached out his hands, and He gave me the world!

George Wentz
Sturgeon Bay, WI

Baseball

In the middle of the street
a sewer cover,
home plate.

A puffy grey softball
tearing at the seams
whacked by a Louisville slugger;

The sound of a wooden bat
dropped on hot asphalt—
Dayton Street;

"No chippin' in for broken windows!"
declared before every game
didn't save me;

The man said the windshield
of his Studebaker was cracked,
"Did you do it?" he asked;

I had a chance to lie
but didn't—
I hit a homer that day!

Kathy McHugh
Ogunquit, ME

My Mom and Dad Remembrance

It's not easy saying goodbye to your best friends in the world whom you've known all your life and half of theirs—your parents, like a trusted institution always there, good times and bad, no matter what. You know someday it will happen, but it's hard to believe that their time of departure has, or ever could arrive. I remember when I used to thank them for all they did, and Dad would say, "Someday you'll be helping us, Kath." While there were positives like my finally being entrusted to take the reins and move about freely without being cautioned, these were far outweighed by the loss of their steadfast presence that I may never get over; such gifted and irreplaceable role models with numerous traditions, legacies, gifts and talents.

My mother excelled in storytelling, humorous expressions, embroidery, knitting, crocheting, quilting, cake decorating, cooking, crafts, music, ceramics, and sewing. The evidence is a sign on her sewing room wall: "She who dies with the most fabric wins." And believe me—she is definitely in the lead! It is my hope that all the pieces of my mother's life come together for us like one big quilt of memories to ponder, share and commemorate.

My father's gifts include constructing a camp, transforming a rundown red deck into an enclosed porch, furnace installation, plumbing, electronics, auto mechanics, and developing film in his darkroom. He was a bomber pilot in World War II, a ham radio operator, worked thirty-five years for New England Telephone where "the system was the solution," and installed the first telephone on Mount Washington. He fixed cars and tractors, televisions in the basement, and in later years he prints digital photos, repairs computers by swapping/recycling parts, enjoys chatting on his computer user's group, completing a "Wonder Word" puzzle in the

Kathy McHugh
Ogunquit, ME

newspaper and a jigsaw puzzle on the table. I bet that God will have my father set him up an internet connection so we can always keep in touch.

There are so many great stories from Mom and Dad's life together, such as the shed that blew across the neighbor's lawn, the noisy diesel Buick, meeting Robert Frost and Mrs. Martin Luther King, cooking spaghetti in a pressure cooker, the burnt pork chops, being greeted by a spider in a Florida cupboard, the retirement cake mishap and the tall wedding cake near-mishap, their car being stripped of parts in front of their eyes, my mother leaning on a freshly painted pole in an airport and their going to sleep following warnings of the world coming to an end on the nightly news, only to be unexpectedly awakened by a rumbling train on a track just outside their window at five in the morning.

So where did all the time go, and where do we go from here? It's not going to be easy, but God moves us on from generation to generation, and I'm up to bat now. It seems like only yesterday when I witnessed my parents helping their parents. But the many acts of kindness and generosity my parents taught and shared by their example will live on forever in the hearts of those who care...This is K1API; over and out...

Robert B. Moreland
Pleasant Prairie, WI

In the Breech

In loving memory of
Pharmacist Mate 1st Class "Doc" Robert Dan Law, II
1st Battalion 1st Marine Raiders H&E Company

Sometimes when life gets hard, I think of you
twenty one, Navy Corpsman among
all those Marines trying hard to eschew
the fear lurking below the surface unsung.

It took the sergeant's leg, when the shell hit,
laying out six more, most of them in shock.
Bullets over your head, you grabbed your kit
battlefield amputation, bandaged, took stock.

Each in turn treated, without thought you stayed
Guam's August heat, "did your job," imbue.
Valor is not the absence of fear. Afraid,
you go because someone is counting on you.

My uncle whose name I share you impart
honor as I remember you in my heart.

Ellen Sander
Belfast, ME

Barrier's Reef

      frosted halo
      winter moon

lost conversational vines
      helpless in
ancient hemlocks hang
on splintery crags

I fade cringing
my colorless spirit
in a tropical rainforest
craving nickel plated daytime sky &
      mute coats walking
on the concrete tundra

a bloodless pierce of
red chrysanthemums
nod through the crosswalk
in a paced fist

tears crisscross
mounded cheeks, riverlets
changing paths in the
calisthenics of a crumbling smile

Irene Zimmerman
Greenfield, WI

Winter Walk

The swish-swish of my down coat
slices the road's icy silence.

Along the fence, tufts of grass
straggle above the snow
to pick the wind's teeth.
In the field, broken cornstalks
stab at crusty mounds.

A caucus of crows shatters
the stillness of the slate sky.
They settle down again
across the road, in cherry trees
hunched against the cold.

My mind slows
to winter pace.
Disconnected thoughts
drift like ice floes
broken off from shore.

Only my breath aspires
to warm a world beyond itself.

P. C. Moorehead
North Lake, WI

Cheer

Infrequent sun,
you are here today
for a brief moment
in time.

Infrequent sun,
you are here,
in this land,
in my heart.

Infrequent sun,
you cheer me, here.

***

Diving

I dive
deep
into you.

I dive
and know
you.

Diving deep,
I learn
anew

the deepest you

Bundy H. Boit
Penobscot, ME

Winged Horse

October winds rattled the windows of the century-and-a-half-old Maine farmhouse. Ill-tempered parental voices half-muffled the insistent thrumming of the panes. A short time later, the bullying flock of romneys and suffolks shouldered their way to the grain feeder at the sound of the man's voice and the shaken metal bucket.

"See you later, honey. Make me proud today."

"Bye, Pops," Carrie called.

Carrie threw on her jacket, having stuffed her lunch in her pack, and headed downhill to the Academy. Worried, Neva thought to herself, *girls grow up fast, perhaps boys do too.* She watched from the dooryard as her daughter walked the short distance to school. Once through the wrought-iron gate, Carrie joined her teacher at the Academy door. A slight confidence stirred her body.

Inside, the sixth graders buzzed enthusiasm. Zaida looked at her friend Alcie. "You're going to the Big Apple? My grandmother took me last year for the Easter Parade. New York's like nowhere else. Oh my gosh! So many huge tall buildings. Corwen, Maine looks like an ant compared to New York."

"Yeah! My uncle used to work in the Empire State Building." Daisy gracefully spread her short frame onto her chair. "He was a night guard. I got to go up to the highest observation deck with him!"

"Owen, today you're in charge of straightening up the room. Okay? Thank you." Miss Farnham leaned against her desk to call the roll.

At the end of recess in the season's crisp air, the bell once again swept students back inside. This time, mysterious music oozed into the hallway as Carrie and her friends shoved their way through the classroom door, urged into

Bundy H. Boit
Penobscot, ME

silence by Miss Farnham's gentle but no nonsense voice. "You *will* be quiet, boys."

"She's gone loony, Owen!" whispered Zaida, her stubby finger pointing to their teacher. The alien sounds flooded the space from floor to ceiling. Bart and Toshi croaked their frog voices to lighten the atmosphere, eliciting boyish giggles.

Carrie covered her head with her arms, lying on the cold, beige-colored desk. Listening to the background beat of the music, bum-ba-da-da-da-da-da-da, bum-ba-da-da-da-da-da-da, she imagined she was riding her neighbor's pet donkey Beulah, as they walked to the beat of the music. Carrie and Beulah were covering miles of sand under a sizzling sun.

"Come on, Miss Farnham. Do we have to listen to this stuff?" Eyes on Bart, Miss Farnham raised her slender index finger to her lips. Five minutes later, the music ended. Carrie smiled.

"Now then, does anyone know the name of that music?"

Tom called out, "All's I know, it's the same thing playing over and over. Sounds like it's from a foreign country."

Becca boomed her contribution. "I like my brother's rock music better." Her classmates laughed.

"It's not exactly rock music," Miss Farnham answered with a wry smile. "It's repetitious, weird sounding, wouldn't you say? What else can you tell me? Is it grand, or mysterious? Joyful or sad? What does the music make you think of?"

"I think it was written for a snake charmer," Daniel responded with a laugh.

Tom gestured with his hands, "Yeah, we just need a wiggly snake when you play it, Miss Farnham."

"I liked it, specially at the end, when the music got louder," offered Annie in a soft voice that accompanied her shy nature.

"Thank you, Annie. And what did you think of it, Owen?"

"I kind o' liked it. I mean, the main part was..."

"I think you mean the melody."

Bundy H. Boit
Penobscot, ME

"Yeah, the melody, I guess. It sounded like a dance. I liked how it got louder and louder with more instruments."

"Alcie, would you please write the name of the music on the board for us?" Alcie twisted sideways off her chair.

"B-O-L-E-R-O. *Boléro* was composed in 1928 by a Frenchman named Maurice Ravel.

"R-A-V-E-L. Thank you, Alcie. I might just play this again for you sometime." The boys groaned in unison. *Good music, good art go a long way to rounding out a person*, Miss Farnham's mother had reminded her over and over. She proceeded to write the day's math problems on the board as Alcie squeezed back onto her chair.

The 2:45 bell clanged twice. Carrie brooded over the morning's argument between her father and her mother, hoping silently that Pops would be at the tractor place when she got home. She slung her pack of books over one shoulder, and ducked behind Becca and Toshi, lined up for their papers.

"Toshi, you got most of the answers correct. I knew you could do it! Keep up the good work!"

"You did very well, Carrie. I'm so pleased you like geography. I can give you some extra work if you'd like."

"I'd like that, Miss Farnham." With eyes lowered, she plucked the paper from her teacher's hand, and shuffled to the door of the schoolhouse. Just before the gate, she crammed the test with a red A+ into the striped pack.

"So Red Head got an A+ on the geography test! We should've sat next to Carrie." Tom overtook Bart in a race for the gate and knocked Carrie sideways.

"Leave me alone, you dumbells!" A+ pleased Carrie. She walked out the gate, left school behind.

Dingy wood smoke tumbled from the chimney of Miss Reevely's house, next to the Academy. The old woman stepped out the weathered side door. Her gray-brown donkey, Beulah, sauntered over to nudge her side. One could never imagine Miss Reevely without Beulah, nor Beulah

Bundy H. Boit
Penobscot, ME

without Miss Reevely. They could each sense the other's nearness with the slightest sound or movement.

"Hi Miss Reevely." Miss Reevely could distinguish her red hair, but had trouble seeing distinct features from a distance.

"Oh hello, Carrie dear."

"Beulah's a very pretty donkey, you know it? When's her birthday?"

"Her birthday will come in March. Next year, she'll be twenty-two."

"So she's twice my age." She felt around in her jacket pocket. "I took some sugar lumps from Mom's bowl. Can I give them to her?"

"Surely. That's a splendid treat. She'll smile her joy. You watch." Miss Reevely's silver-colored braids circled her head. Her happy voice sounded like singing.

"I'll freshen her water bucket." Miss Reevely, needle thin, walked with a limp sporting her patched green rubber boots. She liked to refer to her "rheumaticky limbs," but she managed to vigorously pump the curved handle of the faithful well, and the bucket filled to the brim.

Beulah's muzzle felt soft and warm. Carrie's other hand presented the treat. "You're beautiful, Beulah, and you look very kind."

Miss Reevely settled the sloshing bucket on the ground, already dampened by the previous night's rain. "How did things go at the Academy today, Carrie?"

"Okay I guess. Miss Farnham played some music for us. I thought of Beulah while I listened."

"You did? What was the music?"

"It was called *Boléro*."

"Oh, my! *Boléro* is one of my favorite works. My father called that enchanting music his *thinking music*. I always picture dancers swirling colorful skirts when I hear it."

"Yeah, I suppose so. The steady beat...you know how it sounds? It made me think of Beulah walking. You won't

Bundy H. Boit
Penobscot, ME

believe this, but I imagined I was riding on her back, across miles of hot desert. Beulah's hooves kept time with the music." Carrie gazed at the pale face, streaked naturally with age. "Weird, huh?"

Miss Reevely hugged her donkey's neck. "You hear that, Beulah? You carried Carrie across a desert to the music of *Boléro*!" She stroked the large, pointed ears. "She's a listener. These big old ears hear everything, even from a distance."

Carrie nervously shifted her feet, suddenly worried that Beulah and Miss Reevely could hear her father hurling angry words at her mother.

"I better get home, Miss Reevely. I'll see you tomorrow, maybe."

"You're always welcome, Carrie. Beulah and I enjoy visitors anytime."

"Bye, Beulah. Bye, Miss Reevely."

Coming up the hill, Carrie saw her father's tall figure silhouetted against the afternoon sky. Her mother stood opposite him as his husky voice erupted into the fresh-smelling air.

"My games down to Jake's are none of your cussed business!"

"You bet they're my business, 'cause we're losing ground on this farm! Jake's Rock is no place for you, Brian! I bet you lost twice as much Friday as you did the week before!"

"I did not! Listen, Neva! I'm doing what I can to stay ahead! You just can't be grateful for anything!"

"You'll fork out any amount for a game, but you won't spend a dime to fix machinery. That cutter bar barely made it through the haying season."

"I got to fix it this winter, so lay off the criticism!"

"So you're going to fix it, are you? And the Ford tractor? It leaks oil on the barn floor, and you don't do a thing about it."

"The tractor's my problem, not yours."

"I'd go to work. A job away from here might tempt me, but

Bundy H. Boit
Penobscot, ME

who'd do the garden, tend the chickens, the fleeces, and the house?"

"Neva, can't you leave me alone for one minute without blaming me for everything?"

"Remember your summers haying with your Uncle Sid? My goodness, farming's hard work, Brian! But you're making it impossible for us! What about our mortgage?"

"What about it?"

She raised her thumb and index finger. "We're that close to not making it. Maybe you ought to sell the sheep, the chickens, and all your lousy equipment. Get yourself a regular job, like anyone else."

"Leave me alone, Neva!"

The caustic words flashed into the reddening hills. The door banged shut. Carrie bit her lip, and absentmindedly kicked a pebble up the dirt driveway. She slipped through the kitchen door. Her mother stood at the ivory-colored porcelain sink, staring out at the chickens strutting about their yard.

"Are you okay, Mom?"

Her mother dried her hands on her apron with *Corwen Craft Fair* written in square maroon letters. "Yes, I'm okay, Carrie. I'm okay. I'm glad you're home." Her mother smiled. Since she was little, Carrie had always liked the looks of her mother's naturally curly hair. It seemed to go with her smile that made people trust her.

Carrie put her arms around her mother's waist and savored a tight squeeze, with a comforting hand on her head. "Was Miss Farnham back after her day away?"

"Yeah, she's back." She looked up. "Mom, you been crying?"

Her mother let go. "I've been baking just a bit and it's hot in here."

Brian put his head in the door. "Neva, where'd you put the egg money? Oh, hello, Carrie honey. Want to come help me in the barn? I'm making another gate."

Bundy H. Boit
Penobscot, ME

"Not now, Pops. Got homework."

"The money will buy some of the groceries for us, Brian."

"I need to buy feed with that money!" He headed back to the barn.

Neva caught her breath and changed her voice. "School. What happened in school today?"

Carrie coaxed a half-voice. "Nothing much."

"Nothing much? Was it nice…I mean…What was I going to say?"

"Was what nice, Mom?" She again put her arms around her mother's waist. "You sure you're okay?"

"I hope so." Neva grabbed her chest with her right hand, spun around to the sink, and put her hands on the edge for support.

Carrie lifted the head of the ceramic bear jar named Rufus, plunged her hand inside, and retrieved two of her mother's oatmeal-raisin cookies.

"Was it nice to have Miss Farnham back?" The pain seemed to have subsided a bit, and she wouldn't think about it anymore.

"Yeah. She played some music for us, something weird called *Boléro*. Ever heard of it?"

"No, can't say that I have." Her mother soaked the muffin tins that had done their job an hour before. Tomorrow she would take a dozen apple muffins to her neighbor Evelyn whose twin brother just died after a long bout with pneumonia.

"The music made me think of Beulah 'cause of the background beat." Carrie tucked the last bite of cookie into her mouth.

"That's nice, Carrie." Her mother steadied herself against the door frame. "Now, go wash up. I'm going to get the eggs." She vanished apparition-like to the outside. Carrie yelled, her words an emergency. "Beulah walked in time with the music. The desert was hot, and it was way far away from here." Her words evaporated into the warm kitchen air. She

Bundy H. Boit
Penobscot, ME

caught her mother's bird-song reply.

"Tell me later."

Carrie tossed her pack onto the pineapple-stenciled bench, and ambled to the bathroom to wash her face and hands. The bathtub, washbasin, and toilet were snugly arranged against the pink tiles. On the honeydew wall next to the door hung a Norland-Beckwith Oil Company calendar, still showing September 1977 with a photograph of a potato harvest.

Carrie, on tiptoes, looked into the black-framed mirror hanging precariously above the sink as she brushed her red hair.

"I'll be done with my chores in an hour or so." The voice followed Neva, egg basket in hand, through the open door, but she ignored it. "I'm going with Mickey down to Jake's for a short game tonight. I'll be home early. I promise. Save me a plate, and I'll eat it when I come home."

As Carrie stepped from the bathroom, her mother was just lifting three white-and-blue plates from the large oak hutch. She placed them on the lavender oilcloth-covered table.

"I'm going up to do my homework."

Cuddling her pack, Carrie escaped up the stairs. She kicked off worn sneakers and flung herself backwards, angel-like, across the iron-framed bed. The yellow and green quilt, made for her by her Grandma Libby, felt like a warm embrace.

For supper, mother and daughter ate the leftover pot roast and string beans. By the end, her mother's meal was only half eaten. Carrie cleared the plates and filled the bucket with soapy water. Her mother had a library of stories in her head about growing up on the farm in Cotes Crossing. Tonight's story proved her Uncle Rory's ability to cheat death.

The clock on the mantle chimed eight-thirty and the two yawned simultaneously.

Bundy H. Boit
Penobscot, ME

"Why don't you go up, Carrie? I'll be along after I fix my afghan. I have to rip out several rows." Neva tried to rub away the pain in her chest and shoulder as though kneading bread dough.

Carrie's bed was a refuge. The pink cat lamp, with black whiskers, black ears, sat solidly on the bedside table with a soft glow. She settled under the warm blankets and turned out the light.

The phone in the downstairs hall rang twice. "Hello?" Neva listened. "Mickey's taking him to the hospital? Oh, Jake! When's that man going to learn!"

"Your father's got himself in a fight. Get your clothes on, Carrie. We're going to the hospital." Carrie, half asleep, sat up at the sound of her mother's voice. She rubbed her eyes, stuffed one leg, then the other into her jeans retrieved from the closet floor. The striped sweater lay carelessly thrown over the desk chair. In a few minutes, the doors of the red Honda slammed shut for the nine-mile ride through the darkness.

Inside Emergency, Neva asked for her husband. The pleasant-looking woman, with "Aretha Gallant" pinned to her chest, checked her list. Smiling, she pointed, "Oh yes, alcove 6, down on the right. You must be Mrs. Lansing. Mr. Cadogan knew you were on your way, and he had to get back home."

"Thank you."

The corridor was brightly lit. Neva stood at number 6. Carrie glanced at her dad's nasty head cut. He held a washcloth to his cheek, but a puffy eye was blackened shut.

"Brian Lansing, don't you know any better than to get in a fight? You're a disgrace!"

"Don't start in on me, Neva. No fault of my own. That fool Derek Butters drank too much, as usual."

"And I suppose you didn't touch a drop? You reek of the stuff!"

"He didn't like what I said about his arrogant friend, run-

Bundy H. Boit
Penobscot, ME

ning for state legislature. Bailey's a fraud, and he knows it!"

"And how much did you lose tonight?"

Her father's barrage of words fell like explosives on the pristine atmosphere of Emergency. Carrie fingered the gauzy tan curtain. She stepped aside as the doctor and a nurse returned to attend the patient.

Across from the alcove, a deep green wooden chair with a magazine on the seat appeared oasis-like. Carrie sat down, her sneakers tucked over the front rung. A graceful bird sculpture of shiny silver metal adorned the magazine's cover with the words **The Art of Grant Munnelly**. The bird was singing. The dazzling metal strips of its shapely body pointed skyward. She gazed at it, smiled, then flipped through. At page fifteen, a gleaming silver metal horse was mounted atop a cylindrical column. The horse stood on its hind legs, its front legs poised to take off into the air. The metal was sparse, with empty spaces. It looked more like an outline of a horse, or one half obscured in the fog. Two large powerful wings burst from the horse's shoulders. Carrie flushed with excitement. "Wow!" The caption under the photo read, "*Winged Horse* by Grant Munnelly, stainless steel, 5.5 feet high, Stormont, Maine."

Persistent page calls reverberated while Carrie admired the horse's flawless elegance. She stared at the perfectly formed wings. *Would anyone notice if she tore out the page?* Slowly, carefully, she ripped the page free, folded it, and slipped it into the pocket of her jacket. She turned the pages to see more striking sculptures—a bronze fish, a hunting hawk with a hole for an eye, and a crowing rooster. The curved tail feathers looked just like those of Buddy, her rooster at home.

Sometime later, her mother touched her arm. "Carrie, grab your father's sweater. I'll wheel him to the car." Carrie stood up, leaving the magazine on the seat.

Her father grumbled his thanks to the staff. Patched up with a white eye bandage, he stuffed a prescription in his

Bundy H. Boit
Penobscot, ME

pocket. As they headed home, Carrie followed the river, dimly lit by the half-moon. She tried hard to shut out the sharp words coming from the Honda's front seats.

In the morning, Brian took extra time to get out to the sheep that pushed and shoved at the sound of the grain bucket. "Chelsea, Angel, back away, girls. Plenty for all. What's wrong with your foot, Ginger? You battered too?"

The smell of toast followed Carrie out the door to the hen house where she checked the water bucket and replenished the grain feeder for the flock of nineteen. Back in the kitchen, she grabbed the wrapped sandwich, apple and juice bottle, and stuffed them in her pack. The night's prized photograph was positioned safely inside one of her books.

"Love you, Carrie. Bye, see you later." Her mother waved and watched her daughter from the dooryard. "Honey, it's baloney and cheese today."

She managed a half-hearted "Okay." Carrie headed downhill, her mind conjuring the image of *Winged Horse*. With her legs tucked close to the warm sides, she held on tight as the powerful wings flapped frantically, like those of a mammoth migrating butterfly lifting the agile body into the air. Up, up, they soared. The sleek tail floated out straight. The frigid wind pounded her face, and beat against the softness of her adolescent body. She caressed the silky wings. Faster, faster, the mighty legs drove against the air. Girl and horse, breathless together, vanished into a billowing white haze, a ride into bright light where she felt comforted, loved. A love that was seeping into her body. It felt like she was unfolding. Maybe growing.

Inside the familiar gate, she put down her pack, and leaned down to tie a sneaker.

"The bell has rung. Please quiet down," announced the principal, Mr. Goldberg, from the flagpole. Carrie leapt up the granite steps, through the heavy door. With rare radiance, she waited for Miss Farnham at the classroom threshold.

"Good morning, Carrie."

Bundy H. Boit
Penobscot, ME

"Good morning, Miss Farnham. I got to show you something special." Carrie fished out the cherished picture. "I kept this under my pillow last night. I think it's very beautiful."

Miss Farnham positioned the red-rimmed glasses that hung from her sweatered neck. "Oh man! What a beauty! Where'd you find this photograph?"

"In that magazine about Maine Arts. You know the one? I prob'ly shouldn't have torn out the page, but I wanted to take it home."

Miss Farnham read. "*Winged Horse* stands in Rowan Gillespie Park in the center of Stormont. The sculpture was placed there in memory of Mr. Munnelly's father, Peter Munnelly, a native son of the town. During World War II, his plane was shot down over the English Channel."

Miss Farnham adjusted her glasses. "I recently read an article about Mr. Munnelly's Portland exhibit. He's going places." She paused to admire the horse. "So his father came from Stormont. You have an eye for the beautiful, Carrie. We'll find a way for you to see *Winged Horse*."

"Really Miss Farnham? You mean that?"

"Stormont's on the way to the Robbins Fish Hatchery. Can't promise, but it's possible we can make it a class trip for our November study break."

"I imagine the horse flying, with me riding on its back, way up in the clouds! We fly into a place of beautiful bright light. It's full of love and makes me happy."

"That's just what the artist intended. For you to discover your own meaning in what he's created. That's one grand horse! Thank you for sharing it, Carrie."

Carrie's eyes brightened with her smile as she followed her teacher into the classroom and closed the door behind them.

After the morning's recess, Miss Farnham pulled the world map down. "Today we're going to see how Ferdinand Magellan got to the Pacific Ocean. Who knows the years of his expedition?" A knock on the door, and Mr. Goldberg was

Bundy H. Boit
Penobscot, ME

standing in the classroom.

"Miss Farnham, may I see you in the hallway, please?" Her students took advantage of the moment with another of Daniel's jokes until Miss Farnham stepped back in.

"Quiet down boys!" She stood by Carrie's desk. "Will you please come with me, Carrie, and bring your jacket and your pack."

"Me?" She stood up, put her books in her pack and grabbed her jacket from the nearby hook.

In the hallway, Mr. Goldberg patted her head, and led her toward the office. "Everything will be all right." Mickey Cadogan, her father's friend, met her halfway up the hall and put his arm around her. "Carrie, your father asked me take you home. Something's happened to your mother."

Gasping, she yelled, "What's happened?"

Mr. Goldberg opened the door for them. "Mr. Cadogan, let me know what we can do. We're here to help in any way we can."

Mickey Cadogan came often to the farm with his chocolate lab Penny. Carrie liked to throw sticks for the dog. This time he was alone. He opened the door of the familiar black pickup, helped Carrie into the cab and closed the door. He ran around the hood, jumped in, and turned the key. A lurch forward, and he headed up the hill.

"Your mother collapsed in the kitchen. We think she hit her head on the sink. The ambulance people are there now. I was just going out the door to work when your dad called."

"Where was Pops?"

"Your dad found her when he came in from the barn."

Desperation seized her slight frame. "Mom! Oh my mom! Will she be all right?"

"We think so, Carrie. My wife Liza is with her, and the medical team too. She's in good hands."

Tears jumped from Carrie's eyes, and soaked her jacket. "She...she better be all right. Will she?"

Carrie barely waited for the truck to stop before she

Bundy H. Boit
Penobscot, ME

yanked the handle, and jumped to the ground, with her pack.

The team was taking equipment out of the ambulance. Her father sat by the couch stroking her mother's hair. "Neva, oh my Neva. I'm so sorry. I'm sorry."

Carrie stood beside her mother and father like a crèche scene with the figures rearranged. A plastic tube fed into her arm from a bottle suspended from a hook. Brian stood up. "Carrie honey!" He tried to put his arms around her, but she stepped closer to her mother. She stared at the face she knew so well.

"Mom, I'm home. Please, please... Why doesn't she talk to me?" Her father's hand on Carrie's back prodded her to the other side of the room.

"Your mother's unconscious. The ambulance team got here as fast as they could. They've been monitoring her signs." Brian ran his fingers through his hair, but words didn't come easily. He usually talked to Carrie while he worked, fed the sheep, fixed a tractor tire.

"What happened to Mom?"

"It's something related to her heart. She fell, and hit...We don't know exactly what happened."

"Can I give Mom a hug?"

"I suppose so." He wiped his eyes on a sleeve, and led her back to the couch. The woman attendant pushed a gurney through the door.

Liza Cadogan offered some order to the mental chaos. "Brian, you should ride in the ambulance with her. Mickey will follow in the truck. I'll stay here with Carrie."

Carrie stared at her mother's face, willing her lips to move. *What happened in school today?* She leaned down tenderly and her face sank into the curly brown hair. She felt the familiar cheek against her own, and let her tears drip onto her mother's denim shirt.

Her father pried her away. "Carrie, they need to get your mother in the ambulance. They'll take her to the hospital

Bundy H. Boit
Penobscot, ME

where they can treat her."

Neva was rolled easily into the shiny white vehicle with lights. Brian climbed in after the attendant. The doors closed, engine started. Lights flashed. The ambulance pulled away with the siren starting to blare. Mickey Cadogan closed himself in his truck as Liza stood outside watching with Carrie held close against her. The ambulance turned toward the river, and disappeared round the bend by the pine forest.

Liza Cadogan gave Carrie a squeeze and turned her toward the kitchen door. "Your mom's a strong, tough lady, Carrie. She'll come through this, you watch. She won't let you down."

Just then, a tan Chevrolet turned into the dooryard. The engine quit abruptly, and the driver sprang from her seat. Miss Farnham put her arm around Carrie.

"Oh Carrie, I got Mr. Goldberg to take over my lesson so I could make sure you were all right." She turned to Liza. "I'm Kate Farnham, Carrie's teacher."

"Oh of course you are. I'm Liza Cadogan. My son Jake was in your class a few years back."

"Jake Cadogan. I remember him well, an avid reader and a good writer."

"It's her heart, Miss Farnham."

"What happened?"

Carrie wiped her tears. "They think she fell against the sink when she collapsed."

"She's unconscious, but she's getting the best care," Mrs. Cadogan chimed in.

"I'm sure she'll come through this, Carrie. St. Catherine's Hospital is known for its excellent cardiac unit."

Mrs. Cadogan nodded agreement. "My father was a heart patient last summer, and he's going strong at eighty-six. It's the best place around."

The next morning, Carrie was awakened by her dad who stood by the bedside table. He bent down to pick up the photograph off the floor.

Bundy H. Boit
Penobscot, ME

"Time I got you up for school, Carrie. Is this picture part of your homework?"

"No, Pops. It's a special picture of *Winged Horse*. I found it in a magazine. I pretend that I'm riding on the horse's back, flying high into the clouds, into a place of bright light and love. Weird, huh?"

"Oh yeah? A flying horse! Can you beat that! Who's the sculptor?"

"His name's Grant Munnelly. His father died in..."

"Grant Munnelly is it? My father worked with his father at the mill when they were just out of college. His name was Peter. He died during World War II, shot down over France or somewhere over there. My dad said all of Corwen was stunned by the news. They held a service for him in Stormont."

"Yeah. That's where this metal horse is, right in Stormont."

"In Stormont? No kidding."

"Miss Farnham said she'd take us there, the whole class."

He looked at his watch. "Holy smokes, you better get out of bed. Don't want you to be late."

"I'm real glad she got awake. Is Mom gonna be all right, Pops?"

"Dr. Rialto says it was a mild heart attack that she had. She sustained a head trauma when she fell, probably against the sink. He thinks she'll recover just fine, Carrie." Turning away, he bent his head down, closed his eyes to hide his feelings. "But we need to take care of her." His eyes moist with tears, he stood up straight, cleared his throat.

"I'll go see her at the hospital just as soon as you leave for school, and I can get my chores done."

"You sure she's going to be okay?"

"I stayed awake worrying most of the night. But my goodness, we'll make sure she'll be fit, and back to feeling like her old self."

Again, he bent his head and stood silently in thought.

Bundy H. Boit
Penobscot, ME

"My dad told me many times how much he admired Peter Munnelly. He told me he was the most decent man he'd ever known. *They don't come any finer than Peter Munnelly,* he said, and his death was a tragedy for everyone. I know he'd be well pleased with his son's tribute." He paused to look at the picture.

"You and I, Carrie, we're going to take good care of your mother. I know I've made foolish mistakes and I've caused a lot of hard feelings and disappointment. Maybe I've got a few things to learn and just enough time to learn them before your mother comes home."

"I hope she's coming home soon, real soon."

"So do I." He turned away and swiped his red eyes with his red handkerchief. "We could go see the horse sculpture together. What do you think, Carrie?"

"Sure Pops." She smiled a wide smile and looked at him. "Then maybe you too would ride on the horse's back with me."

"Maybe Carrie, just maybe. Come on, now. We've got to get you to school, young lady, so I can get to the hospital."

***

Kate Leigh
Portsmouth, NH

A Thousand Sorrows

Bad things and good things juxtapose.
Literal, meet figurative.
Though a thousand sorrows dog our path,
Wind chimes still help,
And those little rainbows from the old sun.

Diane C. Reitz
Winter Park, FL

An Orange in My Stocking

In the middle of a poor,
cold Kansas Christmas,
God sent His son
to us as if a promise.

In Depression years,
Christmas oranges were for
rich folks on the other side
of town,

but an orange was there
in my stocking.
Somehow, I had
an orange this Christmas.

Hanging from a nail
high atop the fireplace
where coal dust covered
embers—now morning cold,

my stocking hung
filled with mysterious lumps
all the way to
its threadbare toe,

a handful of nuts,
apple, handkerchief,
knitted gloves and
a swatch of orange color

Diane C. Reitz
Winter Park, FL

bright, rounding through the toe
torn a bit open,
being worn so often,
a glorious orange

from such a far away
place—as Bethlehem, I would
not know from where, shipped to
our town grocer—a single box.

My hand held for a moment
the greatest gift of
a radiant symbol, a
precious, round sun.

***

Peggy Trojan
Brule, WI

Angler Kate

She dug the worms,
baited the hook,
posed with the brookie
for photos and praise.

Watched silently sink side
as the knife went in.

"No, thank you,"
she answered at dinner.
"I'll just have
some chicken."

Anne Hammond
Woolwich, ME

Windsurfer

Heavy winds whip the river,
Raise brisk surge against the ebbing tide
steepens the waves
in the slipstream of current

where white caps buffet my bow
and slide along my flanks.
My kayak plunges into hissing seas
forcing braces to prevent roll over.

Can I surf this wind,
ride the crests against the flow?
Is it possible to exceed hull speed to race
with only a paddle for power?

I face upstream, wind at my back
dig deep and strong,
harder than possible,
but I am doused in each valley,

heaved into the next swell,
all effort swallowed by wind and wave.
Once more I aim and stroke,
and suddenly I rise out of the water;

my hull kisses the top of a crest
and I am flying across the surface, faster and faster
bouncing on the forces
that a moment ago held me down.

Goose River Anthology, 2014//76

Byron Hoot
Wexford, PA

When Following Cannot Happen

I look into the mirror for sign
the way I do for trails of deer
to see what I am told.
    I see who I see and know
behind the eyes in a silence
unadorned are where the real
sign lies, the tracks that will lead,
the pawed earth of restlessness,
a tree marked building strength
but not broken,
      and the thoughts inarticulate
which have left altars
where no map has located
any place.
    I try to stay away from
mirrors. When I can't, don't follow—
you can't come after me.

***

Patrick T. Randolph
Kalamazoo, MI

Greenstone Ridge[1]

Wolf's sharp howl
      slices Night—
          into day light.

[1]The Greenstone Ridge Trail is one of the main hiking routes on Isle
Royale.

Thomas Peter Bennett
Bradenton, FL

Midnight Hoot

Barred owl calls,
hoohoo-hoohoo,
hoohoo-hoohooaw.
I call back
eight hoots.

From the onyx sky,
a moonbeam
glints the pond.
Barred owl cries
eight hoots, and
the water darkens.

***

Spider World

Fog at dawn creates
a spider world of webs.
A dewy sheetweb
links grass blades
and girds weed stalks.
Filmy domes disperse
reflected light from
sticky capturing webs.
Tension-web filaments
tether tree branches.
Attending each web,
a patient spider awaits
an insect breakfast.

Mary Lu Perham
Solon Springs, WI

Winter Artist

Every winter as soon as the ice was safe, my friend Hank Thompson, pulled his ice palace, an old Air Stream trailer with a portable generator, to the weed bed where he caught the big crappies. He always set up on a point opposite a cluster of birches, about a hundred yards off shore. One year a tin-roofed wooden shanty occupied his spot. Annoyed, Hank parked his ice palace five feet behind it. A week later, I set up my portable shelter nearby.

The previous year I'd entered the Lions Club's ice-fishing contest. I was 23 years old then, a woman, and a newcomer to ice fishing. After a couple hours of jigging, I had a big fish on the line. Then the reel jammed. Focused on pulling in the line hand over hand, I didn't notice the man who had walked up behind me.

"Looks like ya need some help," he said. I nodded and kept on pulling on the line until a large bass flopped onto the ice. "Got a winner there, I bet," he said.

It was, and that's when Hank took me under his wing. I became one of the guys, and Hank and his fishing buddies, Pete Simms and Lyle Kirk, all of them in their mid-fifties, made it clear they were proud of me. "You'll make a hell of a catch for some young fella," they said.

By January the ice near the weed bed was crowded with shanties and vehicles. One day two women dressed in high-heeled boots and fur jackets drove up to a nearby ice shack. "You'd never dress like that," Hank said. He meant it as a compliment. He had no idea I dressed up every day for my secretarial job at Caldwell Motor Sales, or that I read art magazines and dreamed of being an artist. That was because on the lake, we talked about football, fish, and the old man who took Hank's fishing spot.

"Get this, LuAnn," Hank said one day when we were sit-

Mary Lu Perham
Solon Springs, WI

ting in his ice palace watching a football game. "That ornery geezer had the nerve to stick a note in my door saying if he wanted noise and a barroom atmosphere he'd go to a tavern."

Hank and his friends were noisy at times, but I nodded my head in agreement. Hank being my friend, after all.

Pete said, "I was coming home from the bar early Saturday morning, and I saw the old man's truck parked down here on the ice, and a light on in the shanty. Wonder what he was doing at that hour?"

Later that day my dog strolled over by the old man's shanty and took a dump by his door. His truck was gone, so I hustled over to clean up the mess. Being curious, I peeked in the window. Nothing there but a small wood stove, boxes of food and, to my surprise, a shelf holding a pile of books on art and philosophy and an expensive-looking camera. On a small wooden table lay a coffee table book of photographs entitled *Autumn in the North Country.*

I began studying him, trying to match the tattered stocking cap and white beard stubble with the camera and books on philosophy and art. Not your ordinary fisherman.

We had some good weather at the end of February, and I took a day off from Caldwell's to go fishing. Since Hank, Pete, and Lyle also worked during the week, I hoped I would have a chance to be alone, to talk with the old man. When I arrived, he was taking photographs of the dark balsam firs lining the shore, their tips like spears against the gray sky. He glanced my way, and then went on with his work. I sat in my shanty, watching as he moved his camera and tripod around the hodge-podge of trailers and shacks.

At mid-day he put away his camera and set his tip-ups. I drilled a few holes and set up mine. When the late afternoon sun cast pink-orange highlights and long shadows on the small drifts of snow, he brought out his equipment again. I drove home, planning more vacation days for ice fishing.

A week later the old man was drilling holes when I drove up. I waved to him before darting into my shanty, drawing

Mary Lu Perham
Solon Springs, WI

pencils and paper in hand. I sketched him taking photos. I tried to see the landscape as I thought he saw it, as shades of dark and light, blends of curves and lines, a mixed palate of color. The weeks passed and I continued to sketch him. He'd smile when he saw me, but we never spoke.

When Hank and the guys were around, the old man kept to himself. We only saw him when he emerged to check his tip-ups. Then Hank, who made a point of watching to see if the old man caught anything, would grumble, "I hope the old geezer catches nothing but minnows."

March arrived with its sun and warm winds, signaling the end of the ice fishing season. "Let's have a good-bye party," Pete said one afternoon when we were sitting in the ice palace, stuffing down Hank's batter fried pan fish. "We'll give the ol' man some noise he won't forget. We'll set our empties by his door, too."

Hank and Lyle laughed. "That'll take him down a peg," Lyle said. "What d'ya think, LuAnn?"

I thought about the quiet old man tending his tip-ups, taking his photos. "I don't know," I said. "The year-round people might complain to the cops about a loud party. The lake's small and sound carries."

Hank looked at me but said nothing.

That evening I gathered up my courage, grabbed my best sketch and knocked on the old man's shanty door.

"This is for you," I said. I hoped he wouldn't notice my hand shaking as I held out the drawing. He hesitated before taking it, then a faint smile creased his cheeks when he saw the picture of him pulling in a large walleye.

"Thank you," he responded, his voice almost a whisper.

"Hope you like it," I replied, relieved he had accepted my gift.

When I drove out on the lake the next day, he'd already pulled out, leaving nothing but the snow-edged rectangle where his ice shack had once stood. Tacked to my door was a photo of my shanty covered with crystal hoarfrost. An

Mary Lu Perham
Solon Springs, WI

inscription read, "To my friend on the ice, from Edward Penner."

I was disappointed when he didn't show up the next winter. I wondered if he was capturing the beauty of some other frozen lake.

The years have gone by. Hank and the guys no longer fish. But I still do. My framed Edward Penner photo hangs on the shanty wall, alongside one of my big catches—an award winning watercolor painting of Pete, Lyle and Hank jig fishing inside Hank's ice palace.

***

Peggy Trojan
Brule, WI

Afternoon Shower

Rain was friendly when I was a kid.
A low rumble from the west
stopped our games.
We headed home
to help take clothes off the line,
close windows,
make sure the cat was in.
First, splattering drops polka dotting
the hot sidewalk,
then a steady cool.
We ran around the yard in circles
with our arms out like planes.
When it stopped,
we sat on the back steps to dry,
waiting for a rainbow.

Dawn Edwards
Ipswich, MA

A Butterfly on the Sand

Good luck I waved, leaving my tears in her hand.
Good bye I whispered, inhaling her scent.
Come back my heart cried—I love you, don't go.

She danced like a butterfly on the sand
pirouetting toward dreams of tomorrows,
twirling out of my life—into her own.
I stayed in the shadows crying.

Who will she be without me to guide her,
wrap her in swaddling clothes, safe in a manger?
Who will I be without her to show me?
Who will I be without her who knows me?

I laid me down in her young woman scent
and dreamily slept as I were her child,
remembering days of pirouetting,
dancing like a butterfly on the sand.

***

Ann M. Penton
Green Valley, AZ

Little Girl Chasing Seagulls

On the quiet Gulf beach, a little moon
rapidly loops in wobbly orbit
around her more-ponderous planet.

Tiny shooting stars flash in abrupt flight
to some calmer corner of the universe.

Jim Mello
Newport, ME

Singing with Angels

Uncle Eddie died yesterday
my brother's text announced.

In recent time he could not be left alone
because he might wander into traffic
like the lost child he'd become

the only time I saw him
spark back to life in these dementiaed years

was in the hospital room
where my dad lay dying
blessing and cursing The Corps

silent as a stone my uncle stood
keeping his private vigil
with his two brothers

silent as a stone
until Sinatra sang

awakened
his mellifluous voice resurrected
into night club melodies.

one time
he sang with the angels

at my grandmother's funeral

time stopped

Jim Mello
Newport, ME

pure as heaven
his voice
rose through the quiet church

on the wings of Ave Maria
to the unseen Throne
where today the angels no doubt
will add their holy harmonies

before the Altar of Incense

***

Anne Hammond
Woolwich, ME

Decision

Dead calm of dawn is expectation,
the lucid air of unqualified possibility.

First breath of wind is insinuation
opening likely direction to a better place.

Afternoon breeze is an insistent chorus
singing interminably on the ultimatum of choice.

Evening hush is a brief respite,
a final chance to reconsider.

Nighttime gale is ruesome finality
raving over inevitable consequences.

Zibette Dean
Edgecomb, ME

Pantoum

The chickadees are out of seed.
      Arctic sea smoke fills the cove.
            Winter's settled in indeed!

The table's full of books to read,
      gifts from children that I love.
            The chickadees are out of seed.

A fox left tracks across the field.
      The mice he seeks are under cover.
            Winter's settled in indeed.

More coffee's the next thing I need,
      then feet into my boots I shove;
            the chickadees are out of feed.

The paper tells of folks in need,
      prices rise and jobs are over;
            winter's settled indeed.

Give me longer days, I plead!
      There's Arctic sea smoke in the cove.
            Winter's long in Maine, indeed.

Helen Ackermann
Rothschild, WI

Retirement Is Bittersweet!

What could be a better word than bittersweet to describe retirement?   I thought it might be best to turn to the trusty Webster's Dictionary to find a precise definition. The definition perfectly describes my feelings about this time of life. Bittersweet: "Pleasure alloyed with pain."

Why do I think the stage of life called retirement a bittersweet one? Let me begin with the acceptance of growing older. When we took a Baltic cruise a few years ago, I told my husband, "We are traveling with a bunch of old people." He replied, "We are old people." That in itself is bittersweet. We realize that we have reached a time in life when looking back can give us a sense of accomplishment and a sense of wisdom. With it comes, however, the knowledge that the wisdom might not always be appreciated because we are a part of the older generation and do not understand the world as it is now or so it is presumed. I think it very important to spend time with younger people, especially those raising their families to know of their stresses and pleasures. Being knowledgeable about cultural changes keeps us in the loop so to speak. There is pleasure in this knowledge but also pain as one sees important values slipping away. Commitment, loyalty, respect seem to be replaced by a desire for individual happiness and a desire to take care of "me" rather than "we."

Time during retirement brings its own challenges. What a pleasure it is to be free to choose how to spend one's time. The bittersweet part is the knowledge that if you don't want to rush anymore, you cannot possibly find time for all that you might want to do. The opportunities are endless regarding hobbies, volunteer work and spending more time with family. The other bittersweet aspect of time in retirement is that you know that time is running out. I love to read, but

Helen Ackermann
Rothschild, WI

have decided that I will only read the best of novels, not just a novel that I might find on a stand and be attracted to by the cover or a few words on the back that catch my eye. No, now I want to read a review first, so that I can choose good writing.

Each day brings with it a bittersweet feeling, the pleasure of another sunrise and the pain of knowing that at any time life can change due to illness or the death of a spouse or friend. Living in the present becomes more important than ever before. One begins to appreciate even more good health and mobility. Friends or a spouse who become ill are proof that life does not necessarily go on and on. Limits on one's choices are often the result of health and mobility. There is a bittersweet feeling that indicates that no matter how well one tries to take good care of one, age will eventually be the winner. Again, living in the present becomes more and more crucial.

And so I find this time of life bittersweet, but I am convinced that pleasure outweighs pain if I live in the present and live life with sense of gratitude.

***

Steve Troyanovich
Florence, NJ

pumpkin weather

i went out walking
in autumn's orange field
where hyperborean songs
were dancing ahead
on the other side
of an october wind
while morning greeted dream

Celine Rose Mariotti
Shelton, CT

Happiness

What is happiness?
the little bird asked,
he had flown all over the Universe,
he had seen the Mona Lisa,
and wondered why she smiled,
he had seen a clown,
and wondered why he laughed,
he had seen the sun,
and wondered why it was so bright,
he heard the sound of music,
and marveled at its beauty,
he saw a butterfly,
and was captivated by its colors,
he saw a blue lake,
and sat beside a rock,
he lived in the nest of the trees,
and listened to the buzzing of the bees,
he heard a dog barking,
and knew what the dog was saying,
the little bird understood,
what he heard in the woods,
in the joyous sounds of children playing,
or a couple of old men sitting in the park
playing cards,
or a young boy rollerskating,
a rock band or singer performing,
the little bird knew it was all divine,
all a wonderful state of mind,
when one is possessed,
with nothing but happiness.

Elmae Passineau
Wausau, WI

The Snowman

I awake to the sound of falling snow,
   that hush in the air one feels
   before a glance out the window confirms
   that, yes, the snow is swirling about
   with an antic grace

And I run to a back window
   and, yes, he's there again
   waving at me
   and laughing so hard he snorts
He's a jerk sometimes,
   parroting the children's voices
   and then ignoring them

My only human feature,
   he told me once,
   is my ability to deceive
Bedecked in a tattered plaid scarf,
   a Brewers' baseball cap,
   and red woolen mittens,
   he imitates a statue
   whenever a grown-up comes by

Roberta F. Record
Augusta, ME

Welcome Mr. Alfven

Growing up I would hum a tune which was a song played during a black and white movie of a ballet dancer. Years went by when the lovely little melody would come to the surface many times when I least expected it.

One day I mentioned to a friend how the little haunting music number would raise its wonderful spirit to comfort and bring me joy. He suggested it might be from the movie, *Red Shoes*. I saw the movie and it wasn't there. I didn't know it at the time, but I was starting a "Name That Tune" journey.

Later on in my early thirties a friend gave me his mother's 33 1/3 record albums. I happen to be looking for a special song to meditate to as a suggestion from an instructor teaching meditation. In the pile of music the tune came to the surface. It was the *Swedish Rhapsody*.

I neglected to be detailed in learning the exact title of the tune.

The name was "Swedish Rhapsody Number 1." I thought it was "Number 2." My classical radio station doesn't play this piece very often but one day they did. I got the name of the mysterious tune: *Midsommarvaka* (Midsummer Vigil) Op.19 "Swedish Rhapsody No. 1" and Hugo Alfven was the composer.

I told my daughter about this pleasant mystery in my life; she was happy to hear the story. Five years ago I got the CD Alfven: The three "Swedish Rhapsodies" are played by the Royal Stockholm Philharmonic Orchestra.

Thank you so much, Hugo Alfven for placing the lovely little tune in your head on paper. It has given my childhood your wonderful spirit. Today while playing your piece, my imagination came alive. The goose bumps crawled over my body and tears of joy came running merrily down my face. I have come home.

Jeri Theriault
Portland, ME

Hands

In 1990 my cousin dug
his mother's grave, furious
and fast in the rain,
the workmen smoking
next to the backhoe at Calvary
Catholic Cemetery. Waterville,
Maine. All of us in my dead
aunt's kitchen, our hands
holding her cups and plates, our
memories twining and soothing,
witnessed her eldest son's
return, muddy, his hands,
blistered, unused to such
work, but capable
still.
       I have always marveled
at hands, the magic of muscle
and sinew, bone geometries,
utility and beauty—like the "O"
(made glibly with thumb
and forefinger) that says *Don't worry.*
Everything's O.K. now; or the naughty
crook of that same forefinger
(*come here, you*) or indicating the way—
sometimes with the whole hand flat
and open—sometimes with just
that most dominant pointer—
to someone lost.
       I am writing now
by hand—about hands—
how they grab, grapple, push,

(continued)

Jeri Theriault
Portland, ME

punch, pile, fold,
smother, build.
       This very hand
with which I write
smoothed the final blankets, gripped
my mother's hand as her breath
slowed, her fist opened.
You will know what to do,
her hand, cooling already,
told me, as she un-clutched
this world she had loved
so fiercely and handed it,
willingly, to me.

***

George Wentz
Sturgeon Bay, WI

In the Garden

... A summer day,
a bed of red roses
a deep blue sky
all the flowers at once
sending sweet fragrance
into the soft warm air;
a taste of nature's fruit
so sensual
even a blind man
who has never seen a star
can hear the band playing
all around him
when he is in the garden.

Goose River Anthology, 2014//93

Liz Moser
Baltimore, MD

My Mother's Life

Mom, you died two days ago.
You were old, you had a life of many disappointments
and yet you weren't unhappy:
You grasped at life, met challenges of place and person.
Early on, your husband walked out on you,
leaving you with me, ten years old, to bring up—and not
much money.
There were aunts for us to stay with while you worked.
You managed to enjoy yourself—

to see a play on Broadway, you hired out as usher.
You found a relative to stay with at an Adirondack cottage
(you paid by cooking and bedmaking for all).
You demanded excellence not only for yourself
but me, your son. Your standards were sky high.
Most times you acted like I didn't meet them,
yet I knew, in you, somewhere
was love and pride.
At the cemetery
I'm shoveling the ceremonial dirt
into the little hole where your remains will stay

God bless you.

Maude Olsen
South Bristol, ME

March Morning

We awake to a pewter plate:
The scene below of all-white houses
Laid out in line around the bend of the road.
Beyond a stretch of snow in someone's backyard
A boat floats quietly on an inland sea,
Its bright tarpaulins catch the eye;
Blue and orange cast their shadows on the snow beneath,
Stark contrast to the distant hills of spruce.
In between a slash of brilliant water
Dancing in the sun.

***

Moon-Boarding

A slice of moon hung in the sky
Beckoning me to hop aboard.
Promised we'd go riding high
Enough to watch the sun go by.
And on our way we'd see the trees
Dancing in the evening breeze.
Hear the robin, up so high,
Chirp his cheerful lullaby.
Telling us it's time for sleep
And not to make another peep
To spoil the quiet of the night.

Patricia Foldvary
Wauwatosa, WI

Reunion

Masses of photographs
free for the taking
shot at five-year intervals
all the way back to 1952
lie in disarray on long tables.

Rummaging fingers reveal
a hairstyle potpourri:
Beehive, Beatle, Afro.
Blonds, brunettes, redheads
turn white, one by one.
Sideburns and muttonchops
bow to male pattern baldness.

Trim waistlines morph into
bulging bellies.
Party frocks and 4" heels
surrender to buffet pants
and sensible shoes.
Polo shirts and slacks
evolve from plaid leisure suits.
In Memoriam stretches to
two pages single-spaced.

No dance, golf outing or
farewell Sunday brunch
at the yacht club...
just a social time and dinner—
a few canes and walkers
stashed behind chairs—
and home before dark.

Jane Ann McNeish
Portland, ME

Out of Body

I am caught like a helium balloon in the branches of a big pin oak. The tree sits on a hill rolling down a series of dips and wooded plateaus until it flattens out into the little town of South Grenier, Maine. I see the library, set back against the florist shop and the high spire of the Methodist Church, which is across the highway from St. Francis Xavier and the beano hall. If I were in my body up here, twigs and leaves would tangle in my hair, scratch my arms, make a mess of my clothes, but I don't even feel the little breeze stirring the branches. Below, my best wool sweater is being cut off my chest. Heavy scissors slice through the yarn strands like a broom parts a cobweb.

It is early September, a bit too warm to bike in a sweater, but I liked the image of this particular chicory blue zipping along the road between fields of wild asters. "Hey, stop messing with my sweater," I yell to the emergency crew but no one looks up. Suddenly, there in front of God and the entire South Grenier Ambulance squad, are my breasts, flat and lopsided after nearly three-quarters of a century and four kids.

Cars pull off onto the narrow berm; people amble over to investigate. I hope they don't damage my bicycle leaning against the tree. Not far enough out of the way to suit me.

Only this morning, my daughter Anne said to me, "Ma, at your age, why do you need an expensive bike? Your old one is still in decent shape." She frowned and gestured toward the garage. "And what's with the knobby tires?"

 At your age? What did she mean by that? I don't think of seventy as old. "It's a mountain bike," I said. "So I can ride in the woods and on logging trails, places like that." She'll blame the bike for my current predicament, but the bike had nothing to do with my chest pain.

Jane Ann McNeish
Portland, ME

The pain started a few weeks ago, just little twinges. When I checked in with old Doc Borne, he cleared his throat and said, "Gloria, I don't see anything in your tests to indicate a real problem. Maybe you need more exercise."

I'd been biking for years, but I thought some new equipment might make a difference. And it did for a while. Chest pain-wise, I hadn't had another problem until this morning when I pedaled up the big hill on Split Top Road, to this very tree.

As I pushed into the effort of the climb, I felt the pain slam into my chest like I'd been shot. I pulled off and leaned myself and the bike up against the oak. Next thing I knew, the ambulance and all those people were gathered around my bare breasts.

***

Come on, Gloria, come on, someone calls. It might be Timmy Todd who is down there thumping on my chest or it might be my grandmother calling.

Don't she look pretty, our baby Gloria. Gloria, come over here to Granny. And I'm three again, my yellow dotted-Swiss afloat on white lace petticoats. My shined-up Maryjanes itch to trip my baby brother, Howard, as he wobbles across the room. My foot flies out quicker than a snake's tongue. Whump. Howard hits the floor bawling loud enough to break glass.

"Try that again, and you'll get spanked but good," Mama says, as she scoops Howard into her arms.

"Gloria, how come you did that?" Granny asks. And I know I can't say that it seemed like the right thing, considering I had everyone to myself until HE came along with his slobbery smiles.

"You're too big for that kind of meanness," Mama says. "Go play with the cat."

But I curl into the warm nest of Granny's lap instead,

Jane Ann McNeish
Portland, ME

smelling comfort in her Yardley's Lavender and her freshly pressed apron.

That's right, Granny says. *Poor little chick. You come to Granny.*

***

"Come on," Timmy Todd says. Sweat drips from his face, stains the back of his blue shirt. I'm sorry to put him through this. Timmy's such a nice boy. I say boy, though he must be thirty-three or four by now. His mother, Molly and I were best friends until she died last spring.

Come with me, Molly calls. I glimpse her feathery outline just beyond the oak. *You'll be safe here,* she says.

***

"Cry baby Gloria, cry baby Gloria." My face is red. I bite down on my lip but I feel tears pile up in the corners of my eyes. I blink hard but I can't pull them back. "Tell them sticks and stones," Molly says. "Tell them that." We turn to my tormentors and make fart noises with our mouths, then run into Molly's house.

Inside, a gray quiet hangs in the folds of the heavy drapes. Molly's father is an undertaker. His name is Charlie O'Toole but people call him Digger O'Deep behind his back. We spy Molly's Aunt Flora in the office, as we tiptoe into the casket showroom.

"You wanna go first?" Molly asks. There are seven or eight caskets set up in angled rows. We walk around the room sliding our hands over the cool gray metal and the sleek wood. The shirred satin linings look as soft and delicate as prom gowns.

We stop at a white model with a pale pink lining. A little cardboard tag on the front says, *The Camelot.* "I want this one," I say. "It's new since the last time." Molly and I pull a

Jane Ann McNeish
Portland, ME

stool over to the open end of the casket. I slip off my shoes, climb in and lay down on the satin pillow.

"Close your eyes," Molly says, "but not too tight or it looks fake.

"Here," she says, thrusting a bunch of plastic lilies into my hands. She steps back and begins our favorite part of the game.

"Brothers and sisters, we are gathered here to remember Gloria Shannon, a good girl who only cried when certain people called her Fatty.

"Oh Gloria," Molly sobs. "Why did you do it? Why? Why?"

"What?" I ask. "What did I do?"

"Shh. You're not supposed to talk."

"Well, I want to know how I died."

"You jumped," Molly says. "Right off Hingman's Rock into the lake. You and your boyfriend, who was dying of jungle rot." Molly's noisy sobs make me nervous. I pat her bowed head and sit up.

"That's enough for me," I say. "Your turn." I have one leg over the edge of the casket when Aunt Flora charges into the room.

"What are you two doooing?" she shrieks. I jump down, grab my shoes and run out the back door. I still hear Molly's sobs as I run through the hedge to my house.

No way I'm ready for that, I say from the tree, picturing all those caskets. But no one below seems to hear.

***

"Clear," Timmy says, as he gets ready to use the rescue squad's brand new defibrillator. Wham! My body jerks stiffly, then I'm being pulled down fast, back into life, back into pain.

"Come on, Gloria, open your eyes. Breathe dammit," Timmy Todd yells. I would like to tell him to shut up because I hate loud noises, which is one reason I like libraries, woods

Jane Ann McNeish
Portland, ME

and canoeing where there aren't any motors.

Gloria, Ben calls from the dark tunnel somewhere beyond the tree. *Come over here.* He sounds very close but I can't see him.

***

It is ten years ago, several months before Ben will drown under the ice on Parson's Lake. We celebrate our fortieth anniversary exploring a shallow, marshy stream by canoe. Though mid-October, the day is warm as July. The quiet is broken only by bird calls and the sound of turtles plopping from logs into the water. The fall leaves, so vibrant, so rich in reds and golds, seem to shout at us from their branches.

"Let's try this one," I say, indicating a channel to the left. We swing through the breach to a narrower, barely navigable waterway. The trees close over us, blotting out the sun. We delve into one side channel, then another and another. One final shove propels us through to the lake and we immediately drown in color.

Trees surround us like great flowers, their brilliance repeated in the still water. A heron explodes from the marsh grass to my right, churning the air as its great wings work to gain height.

Then we are swimming. The cold water slides like satin over my bare skin. Ben dives under, bursts to the surface at my side. "Come here," he says. Taking my hand, he coaxes me to shore.

***

Come on, Ben says. I feel him reach toward me in the tree. Before I move to him, I glance down at my bike still leaning against the tree. I remember the morning breeze, the spicy fragrance of damp leaves, meadows of pink and mauve asters on both sides of the road, Mozart on my headset.

Jane Ann McNeish
Portland, ME

The people below me don't seem to notice the young boy circling behind them toward my bike. He reaches out.
Come with me, Ben calls.
No, I say. *Not yet.*

***

"I'm getting a pulse," Timmy Todd says. I grab his hand, try to hold on. "Her lips are moving." Timmy leans close. His ear is next to my mouth. I fire words like darts into the narrow passage leading to his brain.
"My bike," I gasp. Get- that- kid- away- from- my- bike."

***

Hannah Fox Trowbridge
Harpswell, ME

Crow

Your antics make me laugh.
The latest, hard to believe.
You stand under the suet.
Beak pointed up, straining.
Like a little kid ready to leap,
you give three get-set hops,
fly up, wings flapping madly
and with quick hectic pecks,
knock down your quarry pieces,
gobble them all,
hungrily look up again.

Kate Leigh
Portsmouth, NH

Alaska: Summer Solstice

Alaska, you yawned and swallowed my brother,
Seduced him one distant summer,
On your in-drawn tide.
Tethered in Fairbanks, married, raised a family.
My young daughter dared venture
Past your jawbone door.
A morsel of untamed, inside Aleutian,
She found a dog and a cabin,
Girl-child of the north.
Your wildflowers accelerate under light
Nature wrestles her claim each day
Of long summer sun.
Inch by inch you stake a plan for next winter.
You may stay but you must survive,
Toughened by seasons.

Alaska, like your visiting queen, I watched
The gallant sun drop to his knee,
Knighted by worship,
Then to his fiery feet again, the earth aimed
Directly at omniscient sun.
The feisty rabble,
Build a bonfire, fed with slabs of cast-off wood,
An offering, old wood and wine,
Watch your longest day,
In unscripted reverence on your palace floor
Of ice-toned, black-lichened rock shards.
Time is all we've known.
Our impromptu dance, activated with fire,
Is scuffled hurried hieroglyphs,
Ends are meaningless.

Steve Troyanovich
Florence, NJ

you had already gone...

for Bruce Epler

> **And yet I swear**
> **I love this earth**
> **that scars and scalds,**
> **that burns my feet.**
>
> *—Gregory Orr*

we expected to see you
come out from the old farmhouse
to greet us
as you had done so many times before...
but you had already gone

we walked Moonstone Beach
seeking to find
from what direction your smile would come...
but you had already gone

within the final embers of a late afternoon
we waited (*Apple Jack* in hand)
to toast you at the General Stanton Inn...
but you had already gone

down that familiar Charlestown street
we retraced memories to The Cove
like bolts of rainbows
guiding us on our way...
but you had already gone

Steve Troyanovich
Florence, NJ

the empty night cried into the rain
perhaps in grief
perhaps against the gloom
of losing its solitary friend...
but you had already gone

back to Moonstone Beach
where Galapagos wraiths
caressed your shadow
transfixing hearts
on that ethereal beach...
but you had already gone

back to the farmhouse
a final farewell
your ashes forever wedded
to the soil you loved to till
(under the gardener's tree
a voyager's stone)
we came to say goodbye...
you had already gone

Robert B. Moreland
Pleasant Prairie, WI

Crossroads

*For Hans Josef Freischeim II
on receiving his Eagle Scout Rank*

We waited for this day hoping it would come;
years and hard work distilled into this moment
that passes too quickly, ribbons pinned, sum
of parts complete, ever changed, new imprint.

Enjoy. Recall each requirement completed
in ragged Scout books and sheets when your dad
and mom urged you on. Memories secreted,
store this snapshot in your heart and be glad.

Prepare for your bright future. You must choose
who you will be, how you will live, giving back
or not the gift given you. Law and oath, use
them; without regrets serve God without lack.

Remember who you are, why it matters; save
all those who will follow. Stand and be brave.

Taylor Leddin
Frankfort, IL

Lights Out

Worry had started setting into Kelly Prescott's heart in the last few weeks. It wasn't because she was at a crossroads of what she wanted to do with her life and it wasn't because she was about to graduate college in a few months. It was because her boyfriend, and first love of her life, had been incredibly distant the past few weeks.

Since the day they met, Kelly knew that John Shane was the man that she would one day call her husband. They began dating in high school and were able to keep the relationship going as they went away to the same university. From the outside it was all planned out; John was going to continue his education at Preston Medical College while Kelly was going to pursue her goal of becoming a journalist. On the inside, though, Kelly was fearful that they might not make it in the long run.

This was due to the irritated energy John had been giving off for the past month. He wasn't calling as much and was practically silent during anytime that they spent together. Kelly couldn't help but wonder if this was the beginning of the end.

Kelly and John were walking back from a date at the restaurant where John had once given Kelly a promise ring. Tonight, however, there was a distinct tension in the air.

"Is everything okay?" asked Kelly. "You were pretty quiet at dinner."

John threw her a quick glance and replied, defensively, "I'm fine...I just had a long day."

The two were walking past a baseball field where they had spent many school days and summer nights when they were younger, but now that was a distant memory.

"Okay, sorry," said Kelly.

She slowed her walking and looked over at the bleachers.

Taylor Leddin
Frankfort, IL

A small smile came over her face.

"Remember that time we came here for your brother's baseball game? You got so worked up over an out that the ump had to kick you out of the stadium," she laughed softly, in an attempt to lighten the mood.

John rolled his eyes. "That guy was a complete idiot. Someone had to call him out on it."

Kelly shrugged at his response. "Well...it was a long time ago. You should probably just let it go."

"Then why'd you bring it up?" John shot back, irritated.

They continue walking as John checks his watch under the light of the stadium. Unknowingly, both John and Kelly feel a pang of sadness as they hear a train whistle in the distance, reminding them of what else is out there in a world neither of them had seen much of.

Kelly looks up at the stars as she continues to try to alleviate the tension between the couple.

"If you could have anything in the world," she began, "what would it be?"

John thought momentarily before responding.

"I don't know," he started. "When I was young, I always envisioned myself finishing medical school, opening my own practice, and starting a family with the right girl."

Kelly looked up at him.

"Do you think that's in the cards for us?" she asked.

"Do you?" he responded.

"Well, we've been together for almost eight years, so obviously I've thought about it."

John nods as he once again checks his watch.

"What do you keep checking your watch for?" Kelly finally wondered aloud.

John looked at the lights that lined the stadium and pointed in their direction.

"These lights are on a timer," he said. "They go off automatically at ten o'clock every night. I'm just keeping an eye out for it."

Taylor Leddin
Frankfort, IL

Kelly nodded, unsure of why that mattered. She was still focused on his response to her earlier question about what he wanted in life. Why, after all this time and with no change in the dynamic of their relationship, was he being so odd about their future?

"You didn't really give me an answer," said Kelly, sternly.

"I just told you they're on a timer and..." John started.

"Not about that," Kelly interrupted. "You said you envisioned yourself starting a family with the right girl. What you neglected to mention was whether or not you think that girl is me," she said with a slight edge to her voice.

"Is it necessary to figure that out right now?" John shot back.

"Well it would be nice to have some indication towards where this is headed," she replied. "I mean for goodness sake, we've been together since we were practically kids and you've barely put any effort to make me think that you would want to marry me."

"Haven't put forth any effort!?" John asked, with annoyed excitement in his voice. "Who the hell do you think put that promise ring on your finger?"

"Yeah, and you haven't said a word about what it means since you gave it to me two years ago!" Kelly stated.

John put his hand to his head and rubbed his eyes, looking defeated.

"Where is this even coming from?" he shouted.

"It's coming from the fact that I've put forth so much of my time and energy towards this relationship and I'm starting to think that you don't feel the same way anymore," she replied with tears starting to fill her eyes.

"Don't feel the same way? What do you want from me, Kelly?" he demanded.

Kelly threw her arms in the air and they fell back to her side. Her pent up worry and anger finally began to come to the surface.

"I want you to put forth some sort of effort to make me

Taylor Leddin
Frankfort, IL

think you care about this relationship!" she yelled.

"You think I don't care about this relationship?" he pressed with a hint of annoyed amusement in his voice.

"Not half as much as I do."

"Oh you have *got* to be kidding me," he scoffed.

Kelly looked at him in confusion. She couldn't understand why the man she had known and loved for years was putting her through such a roller coaster towards "happily ever after."

"You've been extremely distant, you haven't taken any interest in what's going on in my life, and you constantly make me feel like I'm not good enough for you," she confessed.

"Not good enough for me?" he asked. "Kelly I think that you're *too* good for me."

She raised an eyebrow at him, almost not recognizing the person she was talking to.

"So your plan is to shut me out and to make me think that you don't care about me?"

"Ugh, it's not that," said John.

He walked over to the bleachers and sat down, putting his hand to his forehead. Kelly stood still as she watched him walk off.

"It's that...I didn't get into Preston. All of my effort and hard work didn't pay off so who the hell knows what kind of future I'll have now," he confessed.

Kelly paused to take in what she had just been told. She then walked over to sit next to him.

"Why didn't you say anything?" she asked, quietly.

"Why do you think?" he responded. "I figured you'd be disappointed in me."

"Disappointed? Honey, you tried your hardest and worked as best as you could. There is no way I could be disappointed in that," she paused. "Maybe this is a blessing in disguise. Especially since you didn't want to be a doctor anyway..."

Taylor Leddin
Frankfort, IL

John shrugged. "Well I thought I could maybe make my father proud if I made it all the way."

"He is proud of you," she encouraged. "He just has a hard time showing it."

John laughed quietly. "No wonder I have such a difficult time showing emotion."

The two of them sat there quietly as they both reflected on this conversation and their future. Kelly finally decided to break the ice and ease the tension.

"So, back to my question from earlier," she started. "If you could really have anything in the world, what would it be?"

John thought for a moment before responding.

"What I really want is to get out of this town."

Kelly looked up at the sky before looking back at John.

"So why don't we?" she replied. "The only thing keeping us here is our families. And we could get jobs anywhere. What's stopping us?"

"Are you serious?" John asked.

"Yes! We have nothing tying us to this place other than dysfunctional familial roots. Why don't we just start some place new."

"You'd really go for that?" John smiled.

Kelly took his hand and as she looked straight into his eyes said, "In a heartbeat."

The couple sat on the bleachers, silently looking forward to their brand new future as the lights on the field softly went out.

Carolyn Locke
Troy, ME

An Owl in February

Last night I dreamed an owl
calling under the full moon—

who-who-who-whoooooo
who-who-who-whoooooo—

and felt the shiver of a mouse
as it skittered over the snow,

a dark shadow descending,
sharp claws sinking into flesh—

then the whoosh of rising wings—
who-who-who-whoooooo—

Come morning, only a filigree
of feather and tail mars the snow.

Mary Jo Balistreri
Genesee Depot, WI

Portrait of Tennessee Walking Horse

I study your large head, your mane silvered
with age. In your warm brown eyes, time
dissolves as I reach back beyond the accident,

and you become breath of sun-scorched hay,
nuzzle against my arm, lick of tongue on my hand.
You lip apple wedges from my palm, and I listen
to the chew and crunch. I meet your steady gaze
on my face like a small *thank you* between us.

Standing now before you, in silence,
the canter of hooves across the vast and varied
terrain fills my body with animal energy, the power
you hold within, the gentleness it belies.
Your coat carries the arc and blur of summer,
the scent of clover wafts around you,
and I am returned to earthly abundance
re-learning all that was lost in the fall.

Karen Lewis Foley
Topsham, ME

Grosbeak

rose-breasted grosbeak
like a small feathered nun wears
a sacred heart bared

***

Sleeping with Cat

Blanket heaves, subsides.
Cat, dreaming, sighs in his sleep.
We drift toward midnight.

***

Lakeside Summer Morning

Grey water kept fast
in fog, and shot with silver
light from lidded sun

Pale lake and boat wake
ripples of black and silver
silk dissolve on shore

Maxine Weintraub
Wayland, MA

Wildlife

We had foxes, lots and lots of little foxes. Each spring there would be a den in the backyard, dug into the soft dirt of the leaching field—which worried me a lot. Could they find their way into the basement through the septic system? Of course not, that was absolutely irrational thinking, but it was fun to consider such a Stephen King moment. After all, we had survived the great snake invasion, but that was another story. Back to the foxes.

We loved watching the kits tumble around in the backyard. One morning I spent long and delightful minutes watching three babies tumble around on the deck. They would leap off onto the grass, chase each other around the detached garage—some twenty feet from the house—then return to the deck to play and nip and roll. I stood at the window, not moving, barely breathing, and mama fox also stood on the deck, ever watchful. These babies were still nursing and every few minutes two or all three of them would nuzzle under her, hook on for a short drink and then go bouncing off again. Her look was amazing. Perfect parental patience. You could almost hear her thinking, *Yikes, when are these kids going to get off the teat and leave me alone!* We shared a wonderful motherhood moment, the fox lady and I, that summer morning in the dappled sunlight.

We had driven all the way to the Canadian border for a week's vacation—the goal?—to see moose. And see them we did. Plenty. In Greenville, by the side of the road, at the edge of Moosehead Lake, and just loping down a quiet dirt road near Fort Kent. Back in Kennebunkport's hubbub, alone in the house with my book, in the den at the back of the house, I felt a sudden presence. I was not alone. This was not a spiritual moment, mind you, but some thing was nearby. I looked up and out the window—a huge moose was in my

Maxine Weintraub
Wayland, MA

backyard. Probably ten feet away. Then another, and another. I couldn't move for fear of spooking them. I understand they cannot see worth diddly but their other senses are particularly acute. So no trip to the bedroom for the camera. I just recorded it in my mind. They browsed on some green stuff, hung around the garden for five minutes or so, then knock-kneed and gangly, ambled off. Two huge guys and a little fella. Right there in downtown Kport, with its upscale restaurants and ex-presidents. Moose, for heaven's sake.

And a bobcat. In the backyard. And a black bear, ambling alongside a back road at dusk as we drove home from the movies.

And so it went. Alongside ridiculous multimillion dollar four-car garage homes, moose and fox and bobcats and snakes and bears. We don't own the land. Yes, you can hold a piece of paper and transfer human ownership, have a deed to the dirt, but it isn't really ours, is it? Nice feeling.

***

Hannah Fox Trowbridge
Harpswell, ME

Bashful Berry

Raspberries don't give away
their whereabouts very easily.
In fact, as big and red and juicy
as they are, many play hide
and seek as the picker gets
scratched by prickly stems.
Leaves, minding their own business
play innocent when gently
pushed aside to reveal
their hidden treasures.

Diane H. Schetky
Topsham, ME

Homestead Trail

A stretch of purple vetch
separates us from the beach and bay
where dusky pink sand
lends a violet cast
to the still water.

Heavy rain has battered the rows
of beach rose.
Their pale pink petals lie
limp along the trail
as if a bride
just passed by.

An ugly gap like a missing tooth
appears in the hedgerow
where the bank has eroded.
Cliffs and dunes yield to the sea.
The island is shrinking.
The beach roses are weeping.

Carol Leavitt Altieri
Madison, CT

The Broadening Sky

The White Mountains
were ablaze with golden, green and russet richness
when my father lost his grocery store in Nova Scotia.

    We moved to New Hampshire in 1942
    in a Chevrolet truck with our scant
    furniture and footlockers. My family

welcomed to a new land
known as the *Live Free or Die* state.
We settled on a farmstead of one-hundred

    acres: farmhouse, orchards, pasture
    and woodlands. During mud season we needed
    muck boots to push and free the truck

stuck up to its axle. Another traveler
with a horse, rescued us and helped jack it out.
Among the blue, wild spring Quaker Ladies,

    rocks and boulders propagated the open pastures.
    A moose in winter coat of chocolate brown
    stood knee deep in the ice-melting river.

Startling me, he soon vanished into the tangled briars
of the advancing darkness and left his hoove prints deep
on the wetted earth.

    As I gazed at the evening sky, Mars, Jupiter and
        Mercury
    were visible with Orion, the hunter wearing a three-
        star belt.
    Can you see the constellations that revolve across the
        sky?

Laureen Haben, OSF
Milwaukee, WI

This Old Farm

A drive to the country refreshed and revived me as no tonic ever could. I came home as if intoxicated and tired by the overdose of fresh air; not too tired to put these jottings on paper for the times when the experience could be savored again and again.

In a way I stepped into history and was touched by its imprint. Surrounded by a cornfield, some oats and an alfalfa patch, I found nestled under a Wisconsin cloudless sky, a quiet rarely found in city environs.

I heard the birds sing, really heard them. I saw them swoop down in and out of their own delicate mazes, as barn swallows are known to do. Tiptoeing into their haven, I peeped at the mud-and-grass nests. Their housekeeping wasn't as neat as some of their counterparts, but it was the work of their own doing. Each tiny nest bore the trademark peculiar to the barn swallows, as significant as humans leave their signature.

Back out in the light of the lowering sun, I found the birds playful and even mischievous in their dipping and soaring. They seemed to challenge each other in seeing how close they could come without colliding. Unlike humans, the avian aircraft never endanger the lives of others. They know how to do it.

And this is where the day came to a close. It began with an entrance into the old farmhouse, restored to a beauty it may never have seen in its prime. That is not to belittle the days of yesteryear. The original building is there but in some way redesigned to accommodate living in the waning years of the twentieth century. Demands for conveniences we've grown up with and are unwilling to do without, find the addition of an electric stove, dishwasher, and refrigerator, tucked away in a foodservice nook apart from the kitchen. There are

Laureen Haben, OSF
Milwaukee, WI

electric lights and there is also a kerosene lamp, central heating and also a potbellied stove without which life in the old kitchen could never have survived. Even now, it stands in this kitchen in its rightful place and is used to warm the hearth.

The two bedroom spaces of the original house only large enough for a bed are presently transformed into the food service room and the bathroom. That necessitated the addition of a substantial structure to serve as bedrooms. These are placed over what we may today call a living room, complete with fireplace and bookshelves.

The entrance as well as most of the house is highlighted by the tones of natural wood, stained in hues of walnut. Artifacts from kitchens of a hundred years past stand at attention on the walls expecting a kind of veneration from each passerby, lest the same be looked upon as an encroacher. A corn-huller is the more recognizable utensil but there are others that do not easily bespeak their use to those of us less skilled in their trade, or perhaps not old enough to recognize their usefulness.

There is a television, a much desired window to the outside world, but when the more rustic scene needs to be preserved, it is tucked away behind the doors of a traditional armoire.

In this place today and yesteryear live together comfortably.

Kent Clair Chamberlain
Fulton, MO

Bless November

Black shadow
Atop crescent moon
Near dawn,
Awake our mercies
In Dallas month,
Fifty years
Twenties' youth!

***

Marilyn Fleming
Pewaukee, WI

Yamaha

cross country
back seat of a yamaha
—tail bone tired

Canada ride
flooded fields of sky—
sea of flax

leaning into curves
under the tires a mile hums
—then another

Published Holiday Edition of Brawler Lit
November 2013.

Lilli Buck
Bristol, VA

For All the World to See

And what have they done to that handsome head
With its thick shock of wavy brown hair?
And what have they done to that brilliant mind,
So witty and debonair?
And what have they done to that flashy smile,
That was loved both far and wide?

They shattered them in Dallas.
They shot them down in Dallas.
They murdered him in Dallas,
With his dear wife by his side.

And what have they done to the justice
This man should have received?
And what have they done to the truth?
Their lies can't be believed.
And what have they done to the Constitution,
And what have they done to the law?

They shattered them in Dallas.
They shot them down in Dallas.
They murdered them in Dallas,
While everybody saw.

And what have they done to that eloquent voice
That crackled like frost in the air?
And what have they done to the people's choice,
Who shone and sparkled there?
And what have they done to our innocence,
When we trusted the powers that be?

Lilli Buck
Bristol, VA

They shattered them in Dallas.
They shot them down in Dallas.
They murdered them in Dallas,
For all the world to see.

And what have they done to his lovely wife,
In her elegant pink wool suit?
Who smiled and waved so full of life,
While death was in pursuit?
They stained her wool suit with his blood,
And spattered her with his bone,

For they shattered him in Dallas.
They shot him down in Dallas.
They murdered him in Dallas,
And she went home alone.

And what have they done to his little son,
A three-year birthday boy,
His father's only namesake,
And his mother's pride and joy,
Who was waiting for his daddy
To come home in a couple of days?

But they shattered him in Dallas.
They shot him down in Dallas.
They murdered him in Dallas,
All in the public gaze.

And what about the man they accused,
Who should have had a fair trial?
Who should have had his day in court,
And a lawyer full of guile?
Who should have had the presumption of innocence,
Until they had proven his guilt?

Lilli Buck
Bristol, VA

They shattered him in Dallas.
They shot him down in Dallas.
They murdered him in Dallas.
We saw him crumple and wilt.

What good are Kennedy's millions now,
His father's ill-gotten gains?
What good is all his worldly power,
And everlasting fame?
For when he was lying cold
His dear wife fled to another's arms.

For they shattered him in Dallas.
They shot him down in Dallas.
They murdered him in Dallas.
He came to deadly harm.

***

Barbara J. Dorner
DePere, WI

Semper Fi

Looking down at the earth from a really big cloud,
God handpicked some soldiers, The Few and The Proud,
And they marched into battle, a core of elite,
With The Red, White and Blue, not accepting defeat,
And their message went out and it shook the whole sky,
"To Our Country Be True, To The Core Semper Fi!"
Men of uncommon valor, they fought like machines,
So God blessed them, and He called them
...The U.S. Marines.

S. D. Gale
Prince George, B.C., Canada

A Gardener by Choice

Willy finished worshiping the sun—the only god he trusted—and rose up from his knees and wiped the dirt off his trousers. He'd been watching through the chain-link fence for sometime, feeling its warmth efface the coolness of early morn as it reared above the mountains in the east. How many years had he performed this ceremony? Did it matter?

Since he'd been condemned to die in prison, Willy disregarded time. He viewed it as insignificant as the society he was estranged from, as the crooked life he had renounced, and as the weeds he spent his days ridding from the prison's gardens.

On the clement breeze, wafts of rose were mingling with lavender and somewhere small birds were twittering. He smiled and thought how swell life was right then. Heck, it had been for thirty, forty, perhaps fifty years now. He shut his eyes, inhaling deeply, and tilted back his head until the sun was shining full on his face. He basked a moment, then headed off to work.

Willy meandered around the grounds throughout the morning, stopping here and there to yank weeds from the dry flowerbeds, passing by a few cons and guards he refused to acknowledge. As always, his mind gradually slipped into a utopian drift: remembering the past while revolving the present without ever thinking of tomorrow. That was how he kept it together.

How foolish the other cons were for shirking their gardening duties, he thought. Not him. *No, sirree.* He remained committed—the only one—for all these years. In the beginning, he too disliked his position as gardener, but as the days, months, and years bled together he found solace in the role. Work in the day. Dream in the night. And exist *somewhere* in between. He attained in prison what he could never in the

S. D. Gale
Prince George, B.C., Canada

real world—to feel wanted, because that was all he ever yearned for. Not abandoned by his mother. Not starved and beaten by his drunken father. And not deserted at the orphanage where he was bullied and flogged into fearing the world.

Hours past, with Willy's god rising high, and as he arrived at a flowerbed by the infirmary, he heard a distant siren warbling on the breeze. He lifted his hand and hooded his eyes and gazed westward. Over the coil of rusty razor wire, quivering atop the fence, and beyond the forest of quaking aspens with its green undulating canopy, Willy spied a vast metropolis of glass and polished steel shimmering like a mirage.

The sight chilled him, and he began shivering. Bile rose from his guts; he spat at the earth. He had witnessed this metropolis evolve and spread every year since his arrival as if some pestilence ravaging the landscape. He shook his head, vowing—once again—to never so much as peek at it. Scowling, he hunched over and ripped a stinging nettle from the earth and tossed it over his shoulder.

Come sunset, he found himself roaming toward the prison's graveyard. A sanctuary he knew well. He had buried friends there and one day he would join them. For this reason he maintained it with sacred pride. As he passed through the wrought-iron gate, his eyes moistened. Sparrows were chattering from their perch on the digger's shed. Willy hobbled to the north-eastern corner, and stooping he began to weed rue and rosemary around a headstone.

As he was finishing up, preparing to move to another headstone, he heard a voice jabbering behind him and so he spun around. Loony Sam, an old-safecracker he'd known forty, fifty, maybe sixty years now, was glaring at him with rheumy eyes as if looking right through him.

"Startled me *good*, pal," said Willy, brushing his hands together.

Sam clawed his yellowish-white beard.

S. D. Gale
Prince George, B.C., Canada

"Thought you dusted out," said Willy. "Ain't seen you for awhile." Sam's face was deadpan. Willy continued, "I should've known you'd kick off here. Once a fella's been in a long while—nowhere else to go. No family. No friends." Willy waved toward the metropolis. "Besides it's scary out there."

Sam slowly raised his arm and pointed west. A recollection lurked on the edge of shadow in Willy's mind—he refused to look west. Sam grinned wickedly as if privy to an unspoken jest. He then shrugged his shoulders, turned, and as he limped away began humming a tune of sorrow.

Willy started to tremble as he watched Sam depart. Glancing around, he searched for a distraction—a person, something, anything to preoccupy his thoughts so his swell day of gardening wouldn't be ruined. And then deafening booms—three in rapid succession—split the air like a cannonade, sucking at his eardrums, tousling his hair. He dropped to his hands and knees. The smell of fetid earth assaulted him. He gagged and snapped his head back. The sparrows had launched into the air and were orbiting in a swarm. They swooped at Willy, who ducked, and then shot up and over the razor wire.

Shaking, he turned around and spotted a purplish cloud in the east billowing and rolling swiftly towards the prison; he scrambled away over the plots like a whipped mongrel about to get another dose. The cloud rolled overhead and the earth darkened as it blotted out the last sliver of sun.

Willy stopped and rose up on his knees, tottering side to side, and jammed his palm heels into his eye sockets. Then he thrust his outstretched palms skyward, moaning, searching, calling for his god as if an abandoned parishioner pleading for a miracle he knew would never come.

"Hello, William."

Willy whirled around, gasping for breath. Jessop, a bull he'd known for a long, long time, was standing behind him. Even in the cloudy twilight Willy's rictus reflected in Jessop's sunglasses. Hanging his head, breathing deeply, Willy sur-

S. D. Gale
Prince George, B.C., Canada

rendered to the circumstance he now understood. "Is it time?"

"Reckon so," said Jessop. "Did a *fine* job today."

"I love to garden," said Willy, looking up.

Jessop gestured a hand westward. "Maybe you oughta leave."

Willy gazed to the sprawling metropolis with its flickering lights, to the towering edifices of glittering glass and steel, and to the alien automobiles racing along arteries intertwined in bizarre patterns. He saw an otherworldly ritual he could neither grasp nor wish to in its profound complexity and reverence for an existence which had forsaken men such as him.

"No, Jessop. I'll stay. It's safe here."

Willy then brushed away the dirt from a lichen-covered headstone. And with his finger, he traced the grooves of the epitaph:

WILLIAM TANNER HOLDSWORTH
1900 — 1979
A GARDENER BY CHOICE

***

Ann M. Penton
Green Valley, AZ

Training Exercise

Invisibly-linked, they chug a straight line
advancing as one single, steady unit
full steam ahead, north, up the bay—
four goslings as empty boxcars,
their parents, the engine and caboose.

Beth Marshall Jack
Lake Forest, CA

Obscure

for my sister

You were obscure, not clear,
features blurred as if under water.
Your face floated up
white as lily
unthreading itself from a pond's murky bottom.

What force held you?
A cold cramp, you yielding—caught
by terror. No prayer or thought
could dissolve the curious balance
of your illness.

We mourned your wrist,
tawny hair and eyebrows
matted wet. Your expression remained flat
as those Greek maidens sacrificed
in Ulysses. They too, were flung too deep,
had to appease some mythic god,
calm a storm, secure a voyage for another.

What power demanded we relinquish you?
A circle of white-robed men
crept closer and closer.
Some began to herald and chant
humming their instruments to bring you back
like a wreath tossed into water.
Their actions were so futile,
as if we could retrieve bruised petals
floating through numb fingers.

Joseph F. Gray
Damariscotta, ME

Crows in My Woods

       I walk into my silent wood lot this morning.
I hear only crunching dry leaves underfoot.

In the distance, maybe a half-mile away,
       I hear the call of a crow.
Within seconds, answered by another crow.

A few minutes pass, another call, much closer now,
       And quickly answered by the other crow.

I hear and see this pair every day.
Sometimes, they pass low overhead.
They follow the same route, as if on a highway,
       And I hear the sound of their wings as they pass.

I once saw them land in a big red oak,
       Moving closer together on the same limb,
       A mated pair I guessed.
This pair pass this way every day,
       As if on a highway above the treetops.

Only going in one direction,
       And I never see them return.

I guess they must take another route.

Patrick T. Randolph
Kalamazoo, MI

Winter Flu, Skinny Dipping Medicine

Trying to coax a smile from my flu
Ridden face, my sleep starved eyes,

My brother leans over from his chair
Next to my bed, puts his hand on my arm.

"Remember up on Isle Royale?" he asks.

"You mean the time when I was seven and threw up
All across Lake Superior on the boat?" I reply with
My eyes closing again.

"No, no. That night at Feldtman Lake. You cried out
In the dark—in your small but impressively loud voice,
'Hey you guys skinny dipping?' And then, there on
The shore of the lake, came at least ten flashlights!
Ten hikers' flashlights right on our butts!"

"Most moons anyone had ever seen at Feldtman," I smile.

My brother's wish fulfilled: A sense of comical comfort,
Hidden humor—hiking across my lips.

Jon D. Olsen
Jefferson, ME

Trust

After more than 40 years,
I've had my share of dreams and fears.
In order not to be a fool,
I went through 20 years of school.
I've played at scholar and driven a truck,
Had some great times and been down on my luck.
There are many expectations yet to unfold,
But as today dawns, one deed must be told.
Of all the things I've tried and done,
None can compare to this single one.
I'm telling it straight, without any lies.
It's to have earned the trust
In my children's eyes.

***

P. C. Moorehead
North Lake, WI

Inside

The sky is inside me.
I feel spacious.
The long night is over.
There is light inside.

Starlight, sunlight,
it matters not.
There is light
inside me.

Kevin O'Kendley
Winterport, ME

The Old Dog on the Hill

He sat on the crown of the hill with pine and fir at his back.

In memory he watched over all that he had known:

The children as they grew leaving small toys for soccer balls. The man that was gone, the woman that stayed, when both were younger and things were better and they laughed together. The love, kindness, and the affection of the family. The spring, summer, fall, and winter just passed—he would never see another.

The man that was gone told the old dog that he looked like a polar bear—huge, dense but with a layer of smooth fat under a heavy yellow-white coat. The man admired the hump on the dog's back, which rose in grizzly bear fashion when he was agitated, or incensed, or when the children, the woman, and the man were threatened. His family called him Grizz and though gentle he was ferocious when he had to be.

The breeze was crisp with a tang of a new spring; it pushed against the old dog's ears: the one that was cocked and its torn up neighbor, the cartilage misshapen and crumpled.

The children and the woman were down in the log house. There were tendrils of smoke wafting from a stove pipe, dispersed by shallow gusts of wind. Upwind Grizz smelled the beech burning in the woodstove and sighed—squirrels ran from the back of the house to a storage shed, chittering, teasing the old dog to follow:

But he was too old.

Too slow. Hips weak. In pain. Tired.

So he watched and remembered:

When he could have chased and caught the squirrels.

He thought he heard the voice of the man that was gone so the dog stood still, scenting, listening but it was just mem-

Kevin O'Kendley
Winterport, ME

ory, not real, a muted echo of a time past. He shook his tail with a kind of hope looking for something not there, something that would never come back from wherever it had gone.

No one said, "Grizz c'mere boy," in a familiar bass.

When the yelling stopped and the children had been left crying, the man told the old dog, "Sorry." Hidden in his words was a sadness the dog could feel and a mask of the betrayal yet to come. It was the only thing the man could say since the woman and the children would now have to bury Grizz when the time came.

The old dog could hear the song of the chickadees, crows, doves, and cottony pulls in a thin sky: then the soft hoof-falls in the cedars down back of the house, white tail, two, three, maybe, graceful, quiet, wary. More than the squirrels the deer mocked him in their stealth. He waggled a ratty old tail—he knew success only in his dreams, now.

"Supper Grizz," one of the children yelled from the front door.

The family's protector slowly got up, walked as an old swaybacked mule down towards the log house. The great dog ambled through an open doorway into the familiar, affectionate, dry warmth. One of the four children scratched Grizz under his bad ear and whispered something in the good.

In that home there was still love, still kindness, still laughter in the family that was left though it wasn't the same with the man gone: the woman was tired, the children cried more, and there was less of everything.

But it was enough for the old dog.

Sylvia Little-Sweat
Wingate, NC

Ruins

Before a dallying Tudor king broke
with Rome to divorce his Catholic
queen to marry pregnant Anne Boleyn,
Cistercian monks—habited in undyed
wool—had for centuries kept Tintern
Abbey's rooms as safe as wombs.
At Henry's command, Cromwell pulled
churches and abbeys down, pilfered
coffers, stabled horses in sanctuaries.

Four centuries hence, the Abbey's gray
walls and turrets of stone stand lichen-
etched, roofless in a vale in Wales.
Arches breach a vaulted sky, form ledges
where white doves shelter from wind
and rain. Swallows swoop at will to nave
and transept, their flitting wings silent
now as Mass and Matins past—no altar
but the dark for prayers at Evensong.

Mary Jo Balistreri
Genesee Depot, WI

A Letter to Great Gramma Belle

Your life stretched like the South Dakota plains
as you rode with your circuit preacher husband
through a shifting horizon.
When I knew you in your unpainted shack,
Grandpa was dead. Four of your seven children
lay beside him.
You were old and almost blind. I was ten.

I came to your house every day,
unraveled the strands of your long life.
On the threadbare rug in front of you,
I wrote your stories down, asked questions,
saw myself
as a writer.
When you tired you'd ask me to play the piano.
Untuned, with missing keys, it sounded awful
to my ear, but glorious to you.
        Keep playing you'd say,
so we struck a bargain: you'd continue to sift
through the past, and I'd bring music.

Sometimes, I'd come earlier to watch you
make sugar cookies, wondered how you could
bake without sight.
You taught me to see with my hands. If
the texture felt thin, it needed flour, too thick,
it needed milk. When the dough was ready
to shape you said to me
        Close your eyes. Let the dough sing to you.

Mary Jo Balistreri
Genesee Depot, WI

You taught me how heat has different
smells as it rises. I learned to sense when the oven
was hot enough, when the cookies were done.
I was afraid to take them from the oven but you
knew your hot pads and trays, the magic
of not getting burned.

***

Steve Troyanovich
Florence, NJ

queenkeeper of dreams
for Elizabeth

you are night's blanket
covering a crippled earth
the glistening wonder
on every winter tree
queenkeeper of my dreams
come hold me now
there is no sadness
where you are...
do not abandon me
to the siren shadows
in this grieving place

Ann M. Penton
Green Valley, AZ

Filling in the Blanks

Alone
in the quiet
at the edge
of northern winter-autumn
meandering the marsh

Surrounded,
but I don't see the cat-tails

Surrounded,
I see an absence of red-wings—
no black-birds here between flights

Just silent silhouettes
of their spirits
etched unknowingly
in my mind—
perched indelibly
atop the tufted stalks

***

Sally Belenardo
Branford, CT

Treasure

Skillfully the wind
shucks the perfect lunar pearl
from oyster white cloud.

Marjorie Bixler
Fort Worth, TX

At the Laundromat

"I wasn't a bit surprised when my washer broke down," Mildred Roland told granddaughter Angie. "Or when I found out parts and labor would cost more than a new one. This old shack is about to fall down around my ears. For too long I've held it together with willpower and duct tape." She planned to sell, to buy a condominium, with a top-of-the-line washer already installed.

Angie had come all the way from Wisconsin to help Gran with the sad task of sorting and packing her things. Dad, feeling guilty, had urged her to come. If not for a heavy work load, he would've been there himself. Angie had just finished her sophomore year of college. Her boyfriend would be away for the summer, which cut down on her social life anyway.

Besides, she loved her grandmother. As a child she had spent part of each summer with her in the charming old family home. One of her earliest memories was baking gingerbread men, Gran cutting the dough, Angie poking in the raisin eyes and the shirt buttons. Then Angie cuddling up on Gran's lap in the rocker to hear her read the story. When she was a little older, they'd read *The Wind in the Willows* together from the same copy Angie's dad had enjoyed when he was a boy. Those balmy summer nights Angie had dreamed about Mole, Rat and their friends as if they lived in the waterlily pond in Gran's backyard.

Monday morning Gran came out of her utility room, a basket loaded with sheets and towels under one arm. From the other dangled a lumpy bag that bumped between her knee and the wall with every step. "I'm off to the laundromat," she announced.

Angie, who'd been enjoying her second cup of tea and reading the paper, jumped up and grabbed the bag from her. "Here, Gran. Let me carry that."

Marjorie Bixler
Fort Worth, TX

"Thanks, Sweetie. You'll spoil me."

Another chore standing in the way of getting ready for the move, Angie thought. Every time she offered to get started, Gran had some excuse. The roses needed pruning and fertilizing or spray for some particular bug or virus. Gran herself admitted she'd neither found an agent to sell the house nor looked at condos. Of course, leaving the home where she was born and had lived all her life wouldn't be easy. "Mama's china cabinet," Gran said with a mournful sigh, "your granddad's big oak desk . . . Pieces like that won't fit into a condo. Not to mention my rose garden. It's too depressing to think about."

Angie agreed but couldn't say so. She enjoyed strolling through the high-ceilinged rooms, touching the long sideboard with its carving of grapevines, Great Grandmother's rocker and the little loveseat no one sat on because of its stiff horsehair upholstery. As she passed by the windows, the bubbles in the old panes made animated spots in the garden outside as if elves were wriggling around under the greenery.

Now she could see that the house had a down-at-the-heels look as well as a washer beyond repair. But she would always remember the Thanksgiving dinners, the whole family seated around the long cherry table. The soft glow of candlelight on a centerpiece of golden mums. A crackling fire. The heavy aromas of sage and cinnamon and roasted turkey. Dad's two great aunts, now deceased, petting her. "Angie, our little angel, what a good girl you are." And "How pretty you look." She couldn't imagine having such holiday memories from a condo.

Angie drove to the laundromat. As she pushed open the door and held it for her grandmother to enter, Gran muttered under her breath, "Don't tell me he's here again."

"Who?" Angie glanced around. A little girl, just a toddler, was pulling a yellow plastic duck around the room. It's jangly quacking cut through the swish and hum of washers. The child's mother, folding towels and stacking them into a

Marjorie Bixler
Fort Worth, TX

baby's bathtub, glanced at them with a bored expression. Another young woman half reclined on a bench reading a paperback.

The only "he" came forward with a smile. "Mildred, how's it going? I see you have a helper today."

"Yes, my granddaughter." All business, Gran began dumping towels into a washer.

"I'm Jim Kelsey." Apparently unfazed by the brush-off, he stuck out his hand to Angie.

Nice firm handshake, she noted, introducing herself. If she wasn't badly mistaken, her grandmother had a wannabe boyfriend. He was about Gran's age, medium height, erect, with most of his hair. In fact, nice looking enough to be considered a catch for an even younger woman. If Gran felt flattered by his attention, she concealed it well, or did having a granddaughter in tow put a damper on affairs?

As far as any of the family knew, Gran had never dated during all the years since Angie's grandfather died. The strawberry curls that made her appear doll-like in youthful photos were mostly gray now. Still attractive, she kept trim with long daily walks and tending her roses. She must've been lonely, though, with her family so far away.

Angie sorted lights and darks from the laundry bag and started a load of each. She heard Jim Kelsey consult Gran about a plaid shirt, pointing out that the label said "line dry." Gran gave Angie a look she couldn't read. Was it an appeal to take Mr. Kelsey off her hands, or did it mean she'd feel more comfortable if Angie got lost? For want of an answer, escape seemed the better option.

"Gran," Angie said, "I'll just pop over to the drugstore and get some shampoo."

She really didn't need another bottle of shampoo, but on the street she ran into a distant cousin she hadn't seen in ages. Naturally they had to catch up on each other's news over Cokes at Wendy's. The rundown on respective colleges and boyfriends took more time than Angie had intended.

Marjorie Bixler
Fort Worth, TX

When she returned to the laundromat, her grandmother stood at the window looking annoyed, Mr. Kelsey at her side.

He loaded the clean laundry into the trunk of the car and opened the passenger door for Gran. "Let me know, Mildred," he told her.

"I already did," she said, firm as a rock.

"But you didn't give the right answer." He smiled at Angie and saluted them goodbye.

What was the question, Angie wondered as they pulled out of the parking lot. "Mr. Kelsey seems like a nice guy. Who is he?" she asked.

"Nobody important."

After a silence Angie ventured, "Do you know him socially?"

"No. I met him at the laundromat. He accidentally dropped a sock in the aisle. I picked it up and gave it to him. That's the whole story."

"A lost sock," Angie said dreamily. "What a cute way to start a romance."

Gran withered her with a glance. "I don't appreciate such talk. This is not a joking matter."

"Oh, I didn't mean it that way at all," Angie assured her.

"There he stood, tossing his dark sports shirts right in with white bath towels. All in hot water. You'd think a man that old would know better. So I straightened him out about how to separate colors, and see where it got me."

"Uh . . . where did it get you?"

"Now he wants to take me to dinner." Gran sounded offended at the very suggestion.

Angie laughed. "So that's what it was about. Why didn't you say yes?"

"Because I'm not going."

"You don't have to marry him. Go on, have a good time. You deserve it."

Gran shook her head. "I know what men like him want."

I can't be having this conversation, Angie thought in sud-

Marjorie Bixler
Fort Worth, TX

den panic. It's okay to talk about sex with your girlfriends. *Men like him.* How many horny old codgers had been hitting on her wonderful grandmother? Trying to take advantage of her. There ought to be a law against those Viagra pushers in the TV ads.

"Men!" Gran sniffed. "What they want is some woman to do their laundry and cook them three big meals a day, while they loll about enjoying their retirement."

Angie let out a long pent-up breath and nearly choked trying to stifle her giggles.

***

Next morning a florist delivered a dozen red roses. Two days later, another batch. Both times Gran looked them over with the critical eye of a flower-show judge. The tight odorless buds couldn't compare with the luxuriant, fragrant roses from her own garden. *Worse than "coals to Newcastle,"* Angie thought. She felt sorry for Jim Kelsey.

In only three days she would fly home to Wisconsin and, so far, Gran had done nothing toward moving. Once again Angie suggested that, at least, they go through the house to make lists of the furniture to keep and the pieces to be sold.

Gran dismissed her with a wave of the hand and headed for the utility room. "Oh, you make the lists."

Angie tagged after her. "But, Gran, I'm not the one to decide what you want to keep. Then could we look at condos? Maybe you'll get an idea of what furniture will fit in."

Gran smiled. "Smart girl. First, I'll find the condo. But right now I have work to do." Clapping on her straw hat, she picked up a pair of worn garden gloves. "Those roses reminded me, I need to check mine for black spot."

***

Marjorie Bixler
Fort Worth, TX

That fall, home from college for the weekend, Angie called to ask her grandmother if she'd found her condo.

"Oh, no. I'm happy where I am. I don't know why I ever considered moving."

"But your house is getting rundown and you can't take care of it. You said so yourself."

"Not alone, I can't take care of it. Remember Jim Kelsey?"

"From the laundromat? Of course."

"Well, he turned out to be a great handyman. He can do all sorts of things. Right now he's straightening the gutter over the front door. After that he'll do the broken step at the back porch. He's already replaced the drippy faucets." And Gran had bought a new washer.

By means of some clever fishing, Angie got out of her that, yes, she was tossing in Jim's laundry along with her own. Angie silently cheered.

She said nothing to her dad about Mr. Kelsey, just reported that Gran had given up the idea of selling her home. Sunday morning he called his mother to ask why she'd changed her mind. When he came back to the breakfast room, Angie glanced up from reading the funnies and was impressed at how much deeper his frown lines had become. He looked like someone who'd unwittingly wandered into a bad neighborhood and been victim of a mugger.

"A man answered the phone." Dad's voice quavered. "I thought I must've got a wrong number. Do you know anything about this?"

What should she say? She actually knew nothing about Jim Kelsey except that he seemed pleasant. Obviously smart enough to recognize a good deal when he saw it. And his persistence had paid off. Besides, Gran was no fool. But what Angie thought wouldn't matter anyway. Dad would be sure Jim was after Gran's money. He'd call his sister in Ohio. Aunt Jane would declare their mother had gone bonkers and should be committed. Angie dreaded the fireworks but knew Gran could handle it. She was quite capable of telling her off-

Marjorie Bixler
Fort Worth, TX

spring when to bug off.

"He was frying bacon." Dad gave Angie his please-tell-me-this-ain't-so look. "He said your grandmother was still in bed. Who is this Jim Kelsey anyway?"

Angie hunkered down behind the funnies. "Oh, just a nice guy she ran into at the laundromat—last summer when her washer broke down."

"Good Lord!" Dad sank into his chair. "At the laundromat?"

"Yes. He'd lost a sock. That's the whole story."

***

Lyn Lifshin
Vienna, VA

After the Pewter Wind

and before daffodils,
thru deep snow and
mud, the flow of the
sugar hut, the crackle
of fire. The steam
begins to rise. You
can smell sweetness
in the shanty. Boiling
syrup steam fills
the sky in this fire
glow there is no dark,
no death

Ellen Sander
Belfast, ME

Python Shoals

The office floor creases like ice
beneath blades, her footsteps so smooth
float on sharp words.

The tiny coolness
eels
in the shallows.

After 11 years she finds
it's all true
he kept telling her she was imagining things.

Sleek across dry grasses she strikes
and coils, prey screaming cut short
in deadly embrace around the sand-hare.

Enter jacket
trying to catch up
coins shifting.

Thomas Rhodes
Hooksett, NH

Visiting Tim

When I first saw Tim he was sitting in a darkened room at the VA hospital. His back was to me, but as the attendant turned him in my direction I suddenly felt cold and lost. Part of Tim's face and head was a mass of stitches covering his bloated and discolored flesh. One of his eyes was swollen shut and his mouth was shaped into an involuntary smile. I sat down quietly in front of Tim and tried to keep my composure. What in God's name was I doing here? They didn't tell me it would be like this.

It all started a few weeks earlier when I read about Tim in the local paper. He was a young man from a little village in northern New Hampshire who'd joined the army out of high school. His mother was a widow who didn't want Tim to sign up. She knew where he'd probably end up and she was right. Tim was on his second tour of duty in Iraq when he was badly injured and three members of his unit were killed in an early morning attack on his base. He was flown back to the States to Walter Reed Hospital where he stayed for a month before being transferred to our local VA hospital in New Hampshire. The article finished by saying that Tim would appreciate visitors.

I'm a small business owner and old enough to be Tim's dad. I've never served in the military but for some reason I found myself drawn to this young man's story. I made some calls, filled out some forms and joined the ranks of the world's volunteers. My next stop was the VA and Tim.

The attendant left the room and Tim and I sat there quietly. Then he looked at me out of his good eye and his right arm moved up slowly into the shape of a salute. "I'm not a veteran, Tim," I said. "I've never served in the military." His arm came back down and we sat there in silence for another twenty minutes. Then I left.

Thomas Rhodes
Hooksett, NH

This was a big mistake I thought as I drove home. My heart goes out to this kid, but what can I say to him even if he gets his voice back? I haven't got a clue what he's been through. Only another soldier could understand this.

I sat at home that night trying to watch some golf on television but still thinking about Tim. The phone rang. It was Tim's mother, Theresa, calling to thank me. She said that Tim had enjoyed my visit. Was this some strange practical joke? Didn't she know that her son and I had sat alone in a dark room for a half hour without communicating? But no, she was serious and would I come again?

The next time I saw Tim I brought him a Red Sox baseball cap and a signed baseball from Pedro Martinez. He still couldn't speak but I could see that he was thrilled. His mother had told me what a huge Sox fan he was. Tim and I spent the next hour listening to sports radio at the VA hospital. It was a good visit.

Theresa and I had our first "date" at the Dunkin' Donuts near the hospital. She told me about Tim's childhood, his teenage years, and then military service. She told me how hard it was when she lost her husband to cancer when Tim was fourteen. I told Theresa about my childhood sweetheart Jessie, the girl who got away. We sat there at Dunkin' Donuts drinking coffee and thinking about life.

The last time I saw Tim the hospital chaplain was leaving his room just as I arrived. Tim looked at me and slowly raised his arm in a salute, and I saluted him back. Tim died later that week surrounded by family and friends from up North.

Theresa and I continue to meet at Dunkin' Donuts. We think Tim would like that.

Belva Ann Prycel
Alna, ME

Evening on Muscongus Bay

Give me the evening on Muscongus Bay
At sunset, when the sun's dying course
Has smoothed the waters to a sheet of gray
And calmed the seawaves ebbing force.
Far-stretched the rocks shagged orange with grass,
And kelp in lovely shimmering scrolls
Along the tidepools shine like glass
Across Loud Island's opal shoals.

Enshadowed in the western fires:
Pine, hemlock, spruce, and fir hold bright
The fractured sunset in their spires,
And raise their ragged arms to light.
The ebon cliffs of rock ablaze;
Below, the ledges, carved and sere
Are fading slow within my gaze...
Beside the bay, small lights appear.

Into the quiet cove we come,
On empty sea, we silent, glide;
As safe at harbor, day is done.
We anchor on the outgoing tide.

Pamela Haft
Brooklyn, NY

The Talisman on the Post

On the platform for the number 6 back to Brooklyn
Sitting, waiting for the minutes to pass.
Directly across from me is a steel post, newly painted.
There, neatly worded in magic marker is the talisman
"There is still time to hope."
It must mean something different for everyone who passes
       by,
If they notice at all.
"Hope," for connections, family, the caring of others in an
       anonymous city.
"Hope" for those whose health is compromised,
Where doctors and hospitals hold the key to life or death.
"Hope" for children to add that dimension
That cannot be replaced any other way.
Or a repair to relationships gone awry whether to parents,
       siblings,
Children or friends, where the end of the trail seems final.
Too late to make amends, repair old damage, speak those
       unspoken words
Of reconciliation which stick in the throat.
Can one find the courage to reach down, however difficult
To make that effort, expecting the rejection which has
       become a life habit?
So much easier to retreat to the subway bench,
Imagining the scenarios, and rejecting them all.
There I am, there, but not there,
Disappearing into the woodwork,
Trying to evade the penetrating talisman
"There is still time to hope."
What is the "hope" for me?
What do I wish for, and struggle to find still?

(continued)

Pamela Haft
Brooklyn, NY

By many standards, I have a blessed life.
Others would envy me and shrug off the deficits.
But it is just those deficits that speak to me
When I read the post in the subway.
Maybe there still is time for that hope, after all.
Not just for everyone else rushing by
Seeing or not, weighing those words.
I have seen them, and they have penetrated my core.
I will look for that hope and maybe find the last piece of the
      puzzle.
My puzzle.

***

Hannah Fox Trowbridge
Harpswell, ME

In Memory of Mollie Schmidt
5/20/30 — 9/28/13

You left us too soon Mollie.
We couldn't meet for poetry
for three months in order to catch
our breaths after your death
left us breathless and devoid
of our words. You will always
be here with us full of your
wisdom, rhyme and whimsy,
grammar checks and knowledge
of so much that steered us so well.

Jean A. Frame
Glenmoore, PA

A Child's Prayer

As I lay in my bed I hug a picture of my family to my chest—
Mommy and Daddy; my auntie and my sister;
my oma and my opa.
I see their smiling faces and I ask you, God,
to keep them safe, because they love me.
I know it is scary out there, God,
but I know that you can hear me.
I close my eyes and outside my window,
the wind begins to blow.
I think that is God answering me.
And I know that in the morning, when I open my eyes,
and go into the kitchen, that my family will be
there and they will smile at me.
I soon fall asleep, listening to the wind,
my family's picture over my heart.

***

Barbara J. Dorner
DePere, WI

I Tried Counting Sheep!

I tossed and I turned but I still couldn't sleep,
So I fluffed up my pillow, I tried counting sheep,
But they jumped and they kicked and they messed up my
        bed,
So counted my heavenly blessings instead,
Now I'm drifting away,
Lord I'm falling asleep,
So I'll wish you good night, and good luck with those sheep!!!

T. Blen Parker
Richmond, ME

Thanksgiving

The words to the song are: "*Over the river and through the woods, to Grandmother's house we go.*" That is exactly what my family actually did. Following the single file trail we walked across the Kennebec River ice from the Swan Island landing to the Richmond State dock. Grampie had freshly shoveled a trail, marking it with saplings (small leafless trees) posted along his snow banks during winters when walking was a safe mode of traveling across the river prior to spring "ice-out." Nearly overcome by driving wind and drifting snow in a whiteout crossing, he wasn't about to get disoriented and end up feeling *foolish* coming home late and out of breath again. He wasn't about to tell Gramie how he scared himself that night either. It was done. He would fix it like he fixed anything else, carefully and with a great deal of serious thought. That trail was marked immediately after that night in the light of the next day and every snowy winter day following.

When making a trip together, someone was designated to pull a toboggan; sometimes I'd get to ride along with the *early Christmas gifts* on the Thanksgiving-Christmas trek back across the river until we reached the dock on the Swan Island side. There were years when passing the river was totally impossible, either by walking his well-groomed trail or by boat. We were thankful when everyone was able to cross for the annual family event. Grampie loaded us all into his snub-nosed green Jeep for the rest of the slow bumpy crawl along the one island road we called Main Street. Some years he had to go out with a plow to open the road up prior to driving the Jeep down to the Swan Island landing for the crossing where he would meet up with family on the Richmond side of the Kennebec River.

Preparations began at least two weeks prior to the actu-

T. Blen Parker
Richmond, ME

al day of Thanksgiving. Gramie and I sat at the kitchen table, working through the menu in great detail for the longest time beginning back when the pumpkins were picked. She wanted everything to be plentiful, cooked well and just plain perfect in every way. As a youngster, I would clap my hands when I got excited, saying yes, yes, yes, let's do that in answer to her menu selections. She would smile at me with her kind, sparkling eyes and begin to write her list. Grampie's assigned mission was to go overstreet (to Main Street in Richmond) for the supplies. He returned after his two-way trip across the river, laden with her handmade recycling bags filled to the brim with food and baking supplies he had gathered, following her list most carefully. He always jokingly remarked, *Nearly emptied out the sto-ahh this time, shuda gone over for it all in the scow instead of Swanee!* He must have been a handsome devil in his day. Even as a small girl I can remember loving the twinkle in his eyes and the dimples in his rosy cheeks.

A few days before Thanksgiving she began to thaw the frozen hulk of a turkey, dunking it in a salty brine bath another day. She commenced to have what I came to think of as a pie-baking marathon. I was her "lovely assistant" atop my turtle stool, until at the conclusion, both of us were completely covered with flour. She could certainly produce a mouth-watering selection of picture perfect pies: custard with a crimped edge, cherry with a browned lattice top (my favorite), apple with sweet cinnamon-y juice bubbling out of the vents in its mountain top crust, blueberry with pools of jellied blue juice highlighting the "B" Gramie had pierced in the top crust with a bone handled fork. Traditional mincemeat pie always seemed Grampie's favorite with raisins, suet and a mystery ingredient that seemed to be some kind of *adult* secret I was not privy to for some reason. Might that secret ingredient have been *venison*? It's only a question! She created cranberry sauce by simmering whole fresh cranberries in a well-worn aluminum pan on the woodstove. Giant

T. Blen Parker
Richmond, ME

brown biscuits, light as a feather, came out of that little old woodstove oven. Plum pudding, which had no plums in it at all, steamed in a soup can with both ends removed set into a pot of boiling water. This hearty brown sweet bread required one more component before it could be served, the coveted nutmeg & vanilla flavored hard sauce. Grampie was once again called into action at this stage in the Thanksgiving preparation. Only he had the biceps to stir this confection to its peak of perfection, a semi-stiff consistency to be spread like butter on top of warm plum pudding. Anyone observing could plainly see the kitchen was where Gramie worked her magic. She was masterful and happy there.

Essential to desserts were the ice cream toppings she made. Everything was laid out like a smorgasbord when the ice cream was ready. Frozen strawberries from the store had to be thawed and cut into chunks before slowly simmering down into thick syrup; pineapple "drizzle" syrup emerged after the pineapple juice was reduced down from the canned pineapple. Butterscotch, caramel and hot chocolate syrups were all made from scratch, containers of chocolate jimmies and red-hot cinnamon candies purchased "overstreet" were set out with spoons stuck in each container for self-serve scooping. Before the homemade ice cream could be churned and all those toppings were ready, Grampie had to *suit up* as he called it to go outside to collect thick yard-long icicles off the roofline. He stuck the sparkling spears into layers of fluffy snow in a bucket like pencils into sand, later, inside breaking up the icicles to mix them with rock salt and snow. Those components would make the slushy mixture we used to surround the stainless steel bucket containing the actual ice cream recipe. Inside the shiny cylinder the paddle turned all the ingredients, insuring that the ice cream would freeze. We wound the handle, several people taking a shift, cranking it round and round as it increasingly became more difficult to turn or until our arms nearly fell off, then we were assured that the ice cream was the perfect consistency for eating. I

T. Blen Parker
Richmond, ME

can still hear all our stainless steel spoons tapping like wind chimes against the bottoms of our cut-glass ice cream dishes. The next hour was a contest of demonstrating the various individual topping ideas. Excess ingredients slid down the ice cream mountains, like avalanches.

The woodstove had to maintain a consistent temperature for browning up the 25-lb. turkey, feeding everyone, sometimes up to twenty family members, friends and children. Arranged in an L-shape, tables took up nearly the entire kitchen, a familiar place where we faced each other to share all those family jokes and crazy stories. There wasn't much room for anyone to walk around to locate their appointed place at the table but everyone carefully searched for their spot. Gramie and I set her ancient but crisply ironed white linen tablecloths out before all the dishes, serving plates and food would be placed. I remembered her using the heavy metal iron, heated on the wood stove, intermittently coaxing the most stubborn wrinkles out by sprinkling the linen with a ginger ale bottle filled with cold water. Each person could expect to find a nut cup of handmade design full of mints or candies and nuts with a nametag placed next to their designated plate. Some years the nut cups were styled as turkeys, made by tracing my hand on multicolored construction paper or leaves made of brown grocery bags, hand colored and cut out in the shape of oak leaves. Other years her origami fans laced with delicate ribbons and tiny silk roses were the project. One year we cut out pictures of each guest's head from photos, simply glued to the side of the nut cup, designating the seating arrangement. The pies stayed cool in the unheated room off the kitchen called the *pantry*. Canned goods and baking supplies were kept in the cool pantry on shelves surrounding all the walls but the one with the window in it, which had the perfect window seat for me, the room where I was banished during time out for childhood offenses. I always hoped that there was a freshly baked pie when I went in there from which I could cleverly steal a tasty

T. Blen Parker
Richmond, ME

bite. I believed for a long time that no one would know who the culprit was, until one night shortly after I was tucked into my bed, I overheard Gramie telling a story to Grampie about how they must have mice because she found her fresh apple pie once half eaten except for the top crust. After that, I heard her repeat the story to many of her Needle Club friends at their next monthly meeting. I was too ashamed to ever do *that amazing trick* again.

Grampie would cross the river on Thanksgiving morning, after getting both the woodstoves roaring. At times, I would accompany him, other times I stayed back to help Gramie in the kitchen. He drove to Dresden Mills to pick up his father, my great-grandfather. After delivering him to the warm kitchen where we were still preparing the food, Grampie would cross that river yet again to meet and escort the rest of the guests, towing a toboggan heaped with Christmas gifts across from the Richmond dockside. We celebrated both holidays at once some years due to the frequent impassability of the river for months during the winter as much as it probably was the one time everyone could manage getting together at the same time and place.

We shared our feast, gorged on desserts with the women at last doing the dishes with kettles of hot water heated on the stove while the men enjoyed a ride down Main Street to "check on the deer." The afternoon concluded by us all gathering together in the parlor next to the Charlie Brown Christmas tree decorated with ornaments Gramie and I had made with dried botanicals. The miniature deer atop a cotton ball snowdrift or a tiny Christmas tree with little gift boxes under it were scenes we placed inside milkweed pods. Rather than purchased reels of shiny garland, we used thin twisted vines for ours. Gramie instructed me on how to fold thinly, using imaginative cutting techniques for cutting delicate lacy snowflakes and in crimping tin foil into long elegant icicles that sparkled in the light of the kerosene lantern at night. I made colorful construction paper chains, our long strings of

T. Blen Parker
Richmond, ME

popcorn and cranberries took hours to string with a chunky long needle on waxy thread. Walnuts were emptied of their contents, strung with yarn loops for hanging, glued back together then the textured nuts were painted in bright greens, reds, blues and gold, sometimes dipped in glitter, all displayed so proudly on such a sparse little tree. It meant so much to know of its origin, I loved those trees more every year. Grampie trekked out into the woods for each tree, made a stand and presented it to Gramie. In the fall, she and I spent hours combing the fields for the milkweed pods and vines to dry at just the perfect moment, harvesting the natural elements we turned into ornaments for our tree. She poured through mail-order catalogues to find the miniature animals, glitter, yarn, construction paper, glue or other items needed to create the scenes inside the hollow pods. They were things of beauty, which I packed with such care well into my adult life and through several cross-country moves.

The best part of all the festivities was being able to open the gifts we had handmade for each other. New flannel pajamas hand sewn on her treadle sewing machine for my sister, for our auntie, and for me. A delicately crocheted tablecloth for my mother, a new quilted denim vest for my father, bottle of whiskey carefully wrapped in a beautiful patchwork quilt for Grandfather. A fifth bottle of vodka, creatively wrapped in a new knit winter cap and scarf for Grampie and brightly printed calico fabric, skeins of silk embroidering floss or balls of cotton crocheting thread for Gramie. I was so proud to produce a multi-colored knitted chair seat, made with leftover yarn on my Knitting Knobby tool for the chair where she did her after-supper needlework.

The worst part was the cleanup, when all the beautiful wrapping paper was set into the kindling box to aid in starting the next morning's woodstove fire. Grampie had to take everyone back to the mainland for the drive back home. We were all tired, sometimes it had begun to snow and everyone had to rush before the storm got bad and crossing the river

T. Blen Parker
Richmond, ME

got too miserable. It got very quiet and suddenly the sweaty kitchen and the big drafty old house felt lonely again, but boy, did we have lots of goodies to eat! Most people left with what Gramie called a care package, her way of sending love back home with them but we still had "enough to feed all the starving kids in China," Gramie would spout off.

For years I never gave any thought to the possibility that other children did not live on an isolated island, did not celebrate in such a grand way with family love surrounding them on that day. Ours was what I truly believed Thanksgiving to be for the rest of the world. I definitely miss those Thanksgiving celebrations; often find myself singing the words "over the river and through the woods" as I drive over the hill from my house today to see the vista of Swango Island in the Kennebec River.

***

Sally Belenardo
Branford, CT

Sea Change

Pale
sunlight
dims; gray,
pearly scales
of mackerel sky
overcloud the bay.
Tacking boats meander
on silver horizon, their sails
the folded wings of butterflies
drawing the nectar of autumn's
last summery day.

Jeff Cannon
Worcester, MA

Baby Shower

precious child
affection's promised love gift
hear our glad tidings

let those echoes softly cuddle you
wrap you snugly in our care

let our happy acceptance
anticipatory joy
ease your anxiety about leaving
the familiar habit of your cosmic ocean

travel with courage the journey that
bears so many stories
forgets so much experience
through the passage to our world

We have already carved a place for you
prepared it with all sorts of trinkets
you will find important for a while

yet most of all
you will find yourself welcomed
we can't wait to hold you in regard
watch you grow in the garden your mother and your father
have spent their life so far carefully arranging
to welcome you into the world where you belong
precious child

Anne Hammond
Woolwich, ME

Toast to the Frog

I'll take the frog as my mentor.
Consider the wisdom of his inventor
Who made frog king of the muddy encampment
And gave him hip-hop rule over insects run rampant.

The ribbet song of the woodland enchanter
Swells into the voice of marsh pond cantor
Leading the service of wild prayer
In supplication of all species there.

The frog is the survivor of the bog,
The dreary name-dropper sitting in sog,
The one that inspires children to leap,
Joyful beings with no dignity to keep.

His species is dying from acid rain
But that doesn't alter his resounding refrain.
With few defenses when he sits on a log,
Frog turns aerialist be it sunshine or fog.

Buried all winter under mud and ice
He surfaces when the sun cuts a slice
Into the forest's long winter gloom.
Wiser than humans, he never sings doom.

Trudy Wells-Meyer
Scottsdale, AZ

Red-Tailed Hawk . . . Messenger of Peace
May you live all the days of your life.
> —Jonathan Swift

Twist of fate or the Hand of God? Destiny—I wish I could be
  certain,
or simply bad luck as one friend called it; in the land of black
  ice
a momentous life-changing slip, one frosty January
  morning
in Rocky Mountain sunshine, outside the near-the-slopes
  condo.
No skiing with the weekend-mob, laundry-day not to be,

as I tumbled back in slow motion; sounds of a break, twice,
  both sides of my leg;
a pile of laundry scattered on snow on a breezy-clear
  Steamboat morning.
I saw their faces, could guess not see what pain looks like,
  only feel the pain.
Sounds of help, sirens like music when they are for you; the
  speed of it.
I thought of tears, beyond weeping I smiled without joy,
  but still a smile.

For weeks my imperative need to find the good in my
  misfortune; from my bed
I watched a bird, as I lived upstairs in the prison of my days,
  crutches near,
a road I did not choose, anticipating sorrow; a time to easily
  be discouraged,
bringing me back to a more innocent time. I found the seed
  of gratitude.
Unexpected, irrational optimism comes from where?

Trudy Wells-Meyer
Scottsdale, AZ

In helpless surrender I watched the immeasurable quiet, on
        a snow covered Aspen branch
a breast piercing red-tailed hawk, a dream-quality to see
        silence outside, snowflakes,
a calm world of frozen moments, allowing my soul to escape
        from pain;
filling me with inner harmony, oddly luminous as lit by an
        invisible candle.
To know peace is to know God; nor after, nor ever will I
        forget—a bird of peace.
Wounds eventually heal, scars remain, an event that won't
        change history
indelibly leaving a belief, something is good about everything.

When the nothing that is something surrounds you,
        when your caregiver is Luke,
my love around the corner, food on a tray, fit for a queen;
        a new chef was born. It was madly romantic.
Whatever tragedy I encountered I sigh as baby steps teach
        me to walk.
Will the pain of spring give me a true gift: hike again in the
        summer?
Looking upon the blue no snow sky I winced as if in pain,
        the cold breeze unaware of the dark eyes of the future
silenced by snow—memories of one rare bird.

Patricia Foldvary
Wauwatosa, WI

Images

Flukes flashing, spouting Humpbacks
chase herring and krill.
Harbor porpoises roll in sapphire swells.
The sea otter floats belly-up—curious, blinking—
waves flippery feet.

Tlingit totems boast the sacred raven
benevolent and malevolent creator of the world.
Flared glacier skirts
foot stark snow-veined mountains.
Moose and caribou raise majestic antlers,
sniff Denali air, root for tender shoots.

Alaskans—tough, living rough—
embrace frigid darkness,
carve out snow caves, mush dog sleds,
cheer the 1100-mile Iditarod,
work the pipeline, ply rushing streams
like bears hunting silvery salmon.

Erstwhile gold rush towns
press narrow against rocky backdrops.
Mt. McKinley, highest throne, presides
reluctant to reveal its shrouded crest
above the vast and wild last frontier.

Robert Erickson
Round Pond, ME

The Confession

I saw Him in the garden, dressed very simply in His flowing robe, a prayer belt at His waist. His head was tilted to the ground, deep in thought. His back was to me and as I hesitantly approached I could see how He gently fondled the tall flowers growing near. Fear welled up inside me as I groped closer with mincing little steps. Just think me! Little me going to walk with the Savior of Mankind, the Prince of Peace! I opened my mouth and there was nothing. I tried to run away but couldn't move. My heart was pounding wildly and I could neither move closer nor run away...so I cried. I just stood there and cried. And then He turned.

The instant I saw His face my emotions roared to the surface as my heart forced the words from my lips. All the fear and guilt spilled from my dry mouth, "Oh dear Jesus, how I love You. Help me Lord, I am such a sinner." I fell to my knees, "I am so weak," I cried.

His hand touched my shoulder, giving me a reassuring squeeze as He affectionately said, "So this is Adam." There was silence. "Look at Me and stand, you needn't be afraid. I know every hair on your head as I know every grain of sand on the shores, and I love you. So stand Adam, and look at Me."

The fear was leaving and my breathing was returning to normal as I lifted my face to His. He helped me to my feet. I stood taller than He but we met each other's eyes with a firm gaze. I became totally unafraid now as I stared into large brown, softly steady eyes. The corners turned down a little and their expression showed the compassion and suffering of long ago. His long hair was dark brown and His beard a little lighter. He obviously caught me studying His slender but sturdy features because a trace of a smile crossed His lips as He said, "Your face is full of wonder." Then He smiled fully

Robert Erickson
Round Pond, ME

and the warmth of His heart filled me with great joy as I fully realized that I was standing before the Lord and, yes, He was really talking to me and smiling. Praise God!

"Dear Lord, please forgive me. I have talked to You in prayer so many times. I have felt Your presence often and I have been amazed at Your unlimited grace and glory—but when I found that I would be able to see You and talk with You—why, I just didn't know what to think or do. I just couldn't imagine why I would—why—why me?" I stammered in embarrassment.

"Come, let's walk," He said while He gently took my arm guiding me to a shaded path nearby. My fear was amazingly gone now but my knees were still a little weak as I hung on every word, knowing now that this was real and I was not dreaming. I was taking a short walk with Jesus Christ, our Lord and Savior.

The late day was bright and warm and the cool shaded path was a relief from the hot sun struggling through the trees. We walked slowly, the Lord and I, in deep thought and neither of us broke the silence for what seemed to be an eternity. Finally it was He who spoke. And as He spoke I found something compelling about Him. Whenever He had words for me, He always looked at me with total eye contact. He never spoke looking away. That only added to my great anticipation as He stopped, turned to me slowly and said, "You know that I am coming again, just as the Scriptures say?"

"Yes Lord, I do," I replied gazing into His kind face.

"I weep for many in this world as I wept for Jerusalem. There seems to be so many who don't believe that my Father will send Me again. The seeds planted by my life here on earth have not found as fertile soil as God had hoped. Much has fallen on rocky soil or among the thorns. I will say this only once to you, so listen well. There is a place in heaven for those who believe in Me; I am the way to God. So tell all of those you touch that the day is near."

Robert Erickson
Round Pond, ME

"Yes, dear Lord, I shall," I whispered.

His face softened as we continued our walk. That soft smile crossed His face and again He caught my eyes before He said, "Everyone today has a choice, and it is such a simple choice. I don't understand why it is so difficult to accept the Son of God as their Savior. I am the Way, the Light and Forgiver of sins and My life is well recorded but so many make other choices. I know that I will weep again for those who deny Me. Now what do you say Adam? What is in your heart? Why do people deny or doubt Me the way you have doubted in the past?"

I thought for a moment wondering why a question like that wouldn't have devastated me on the spot. But the love in His eyes seemed to overwhelm the waves of fear in my heart once again. Such a man, the living God who knew every sin I ever committed, every doubt I ever had about His truth. Yet, asking me what I thought about the failings of man. Dear God, how can I confess all that?

"Dear Lord, I'm not sure I know how to even try to answer," I started with surprising calm. "I know that some people just haven't heard. They don't know anything about what and who You are and what You have done. I guess they just live in ignorance, dear Jesus, doing what comes along each day. They only know what their existence has taught them. Living by their social code I suppose we could say." Words were coming out of my mouth and I knew I was talking too fast but I couldn't stop. "Then I have seen some people who seem to rely on themselves, their own intellect and their own ability to cope with life. To be honest with you, Lord, some of them seem to get along all right. They are good to others; they do good works and live moral lives but they deny You as the Son of God. They hear the Word, dear Jesus, but they don't seem to accept it, I don't know, I don't know," I cried out in tears.

"Don't worry," Christ said seeing my tears of concern, "go on, please Adam, go on."

Robert Erickson
Round Pond, ME

"Well there are others, Jesus. And dear Lord, I think they need your guidance most of all. All the lonely people who have heard the Law, they have heard that You died for them—just for them. They know of Your promises, they realize that they have an inheritance coming to them. Salvation Lord, salvation and a place in heaven. And hope, Lord, they know that in Christ there is life hereafter and in sin there is death. They know this is the choice, then why? Why do they fall away, deny You, choose sin over the Way? It is like choosing death over life! Oh dear Lord, they must be driven to make a horrible choice like that!"

The sun had dropped through the leaves, the light slanting in from the horizon. Christ's face bright with the glow. His eyes were still fixed on mine and I realized that tears were streaming down my face. I had blurted out and carried on and on now knowing I was confessing about me, my sins and my lack, not those of mankind.

The silence froze my last sound. The stillness gripped me as I realized how carried away I had become. Not a leaf stirred. The only motion came from the half round, red sun slowly setting. I fell to my knees and looked down at His scarred, sandaled feet, weeping from the depths of my humanness. Again, the hand on my shoulder, the gentle squeeze of assurance and that soft voice soothing my fear.

"Oh you of little faith," He said gently and almost far off. "Don't you realize, Adam, that you are all of those people you described. Each of you has a little of all mankind in their hearts and as they grow in strength with Me, they change. The change can be gradual or sudden and it is many times painful as you struggle with your human desires. But never forget that as long as you have made the choice in your life and have faith in Me, you shall have eternal life. Also, never forget how I love you. I gave my life for you but you owe Me nothing except to love Me in return. You are saved and free, Adam."

Silence. There was nothing to say. I couldn't feel, speak

Robert Erickson
Round Pond, ME

or move as His words burned into my soul. Long moments passed, the sun had fallen and its rays painted the puffed clouds pink. So still. So very still and shadows grew long.

"I must go now, Adam."

"Oh no Lord, please a few more moments," I pleaded.

"No, I must go now but remember all that I have said. It shall come to pass. You must go now also."

I stood for a long moment, taking in His holy appearance, trying to catch every last image lest I forget. But I knew I had to go as it was late and they were expecting me back. I slowly backed out of the garden till I could see Him no more. For the first time in years I had hope in my heart. Now I could make something of my life. Maybe now the guilt will leave. Imagine me—me talking to the Lord Himself. He said I was saved and free. My steps grew quicker as I felt a tremendous weight taken off my shoulders.

"Saved and free, oh thank You, Jesus," I shouted to the wind. "Thank You, Lord," I was running and jumping for joy. "Praise You, Jesus," running faster.

Too soon, too soon I was back at the gate where this great episode of my life had begun just a short time earlier. But what joy compared to when I left.

"Hello George," I smiled at the guard.

"Well it's about time you was back," he muttered in reply. "You gonna miss the headcount at supper if you don't hurry."

The heavy iron gate clanged and the automatic lock whirred and slammed into place. All was secure once again at the state penitentiary.

Russell Buker
Alexander, ME

Apricity

pre-dawn hand
firms on citric
rind of frigid
air

over spiral glass
of elevation,
heights of land,
pooling

ephemeral streams,
record of water,
toward a lower
ground

how quiet dawn
slides down its
sharp angle of
incidence

a tilted sentence
bright thought
with but fallow
heat

Patricia Lynne Janke
Wauwatosa , WI

Fire's Hiss

Dreamy eyes absorb the calming flames
cinders flicker
Laying my soul bare
To scalding thoughts of yesteryear
Emotions flare
Smouldering pain engulfing foul air
Nostrils burning
Stomach churning
Change the channel in my mind
Leave the past behind
Embrace the dance of flames
Soothing heat as balm
Once again absorbing calm

***

Zibette Dean
Edgecomb, ME

And a Bluebird

When the lilacs are in bloom
and a bluebird's in my garden
I'll rejoice in their perfume
when the lilacs are in bloom.
I will fill the living room
with blossoms in a carton
when the lilacs are in bloom
and a bluebird's in my garden.

Marilyn Fleming
Pewaukee, WI

Africa Sunrise

the screech of the monkey
Sunday's newspaper
            still in the box

high heeled shoes
in a brown paper sack
the coroner's eyes

papier mache
shopping for a mourning dress
the same blue sky

my dead sister
leading the procession
            bamboo flute

at the gravesite
so much quiet
only Father's sobbing

phantom pain
tucked in the gentle earth
a handful of dirt

wet butterfly
emerging from the pupa
a bed of twigs

trying to remember
the two of us
and still the dawn

Marilyn Fleming
Pewaukee, WI

Africa is like that—
        a wet newborn
whisked away by a cheetah

Award First Prize in the Hildegarde Janzen Oriental Forms Award
from "Amelia," Bakersfield, CA, Dec. 1988.

***

Liz Moser
Baltimore, MD

Focus

Sometimes we focus on the edges
and allow ourselves to concentrate on
jewels and fabrics, colors, menus,
places, timing and coordination—
logistical minutiae that form a solid basis
for the wedding, then the life beyond.

Although the parties and the people
give us pleasure, warmth and glory
we still must slip away,
breathe deep, absorb
the magic of the coming union
when two separate souls
blend a portion of themselves
into a new creation.

Carol Leavitt Altieri
Madison, CT

Wandering in Hammonasset Park

Above the shore, I watch the great white heron
with gigantic wing span envelop space,
ride the airwaves trailing its slender black legs.
In the moments between sunset and dusk
agile aviators, willets whistle over the sand hills.
A flock of piping plovers cut a dash,
defending their young on the upper shore
running back and forth pretending to be hurt,
trilling high notes.

Alone now, I remember the many times
we explored ocean bays and salt marshes:
collecting sculptures of sea shells,
surveying seals in the river
and once watched a Diamondback Terrapin cross our path.

At times, I close my eyes to hear the Fiddler Crabs' music.
Waves of silence between the requiem of the tide going out,
and the time before the last-light fading.

This is a world that dies, transforms and goes on
under a vast light-streaked sky.
The Hammonasset River twists and curves seeking
its ultimate outlet into the Sound
as air currents going out to sea pass over Rosa Rugosa.

Mary Jane Mason
Larchmont, NY

Jake and Arnold

Three months after his release from the state penitentiary Jake Robbins was having nightmares. Stomach upset and headaches added to his misery. He was living in the Bronx with his sister Arlene. While he looked for steady employment, he did odd jobs for people in the neighborhood and gave most of what he made to Arlene. It wasn't much but it made him feel better about intruding in her life. Actually, it wasn't much at all, and he had practically nothing left over for himself. He needed new clothes, he needed smokes, he needed a beer every now and then. He gave a lot of thought to methods of getting more money and finally the obvious answer came to him. He'd do what he'd done before. He'd learned a lot and had five years to analyze his mistakes. This effort would be more successful.

It was. And this time he hadn't even used a gun. He hid his profits in a long abandoned car in a vacant lot alongside the highway.

Arlene couldn't know. She was so good to let him stay at her place. Nobody knew, not even his best friend Alex. It had been a month since the event and he hadn't dared to go near the car. What was the use of having a lot of money if he couldn't spend it? What if someone found the Styrofoam cup holding the bills? Well, at least they'd never connect it to him. Would they? He'd worn a hood over his head and hadn't spoken out loud. He'd worn gloves. He'd dropped the hood and gloves in the back of a garbage truck the following morning.

He was sick of worrying about it. Maybe he'd done a stupid thing. Maybe? Of course he had! If he was found out, he'd be back in the pen tomorrow. He couldn't go back there! It was hell there. He needed to talk to someone, so he went by Alex's place and asked him to go out for coffee.

Mary Jane Mason
Larchmont, NY

At the burger joint around the corner from Alex's building, Jake poured out the whole story to Alex, who urged him to turn himself in and return the money.

Jake shuddered. "I can't go back to the pen. It was horrible. I was beat up, bullied, stolen from and almost raped. I can't go back there! I'd rather die than go back."

"Have you talked it over with Arlene?" Alex asked.

"No! What she doesn't know can't hurt her. And she'd be so disappointed in me. I couldn't face her."

"You should have thought of all this before you hit that bodega," Alex told him.

"Yeah, I know. I'm really sorry now that I did it. I keep thinking about it. I keep thinking someone knows. I have nightmares about it."

They stopped at the bar and grille on the way home from the burger joint. "Alex, I really want you to know where the stash is," Jake begged. "That way, if I get collared, you can use it and share it with Arlene. Just wait a while, that's all. And don't ever tell her where it came from."

"NO!" spat back Alex. "I don't want to be an accessory after the fact! No way!"

"Well then, I'll write the location and directions down and you won't have to look at it unless you need to," offered Jake. "Well, okay," Alex agreed, but grudgingly. Jake grabbed a bar napkin, fished out a pen from his jacket pocket and carefully wrote down the information. He handed it to Alex who stuffed it in his back pocket. "I hope I never have to look at this," he grumbled.

They paid the bill and walked toward the door of the bar. Jake overheard a group of construction workers talking about the new mall they'd started working on, alongside the highway. He caught his breath, shook his head to clear his thinking and slowly left the bar. "Alex, I have to make a stop before I go home. Do you want to come?"

"Okay, where?"

"Never mind, just come along. You can wait nearby if you

Mary Jane Mason
Larchmont, NY

want." They started across the boulevard.

A few minutes later, the cop and EMS worker filled in the report sheet on the hit and run fatality. "Damn shame, wasting these two guys and right in the crosswalk, too. They weren't even jaywalking. I don't think they were drunk either, though I did find this bar napkin in this guy's pocket," said the cop. "Guess he worked up at the new mall site."

***

Sitting on the front stoop of Lewis's building, the boys surveyed the street below. "Sure wish I had a bike."

"Me, too. Did you ask for one?" asked Arnold

"Yup. They said no. Too dangerous in the city," answered Lewis. "Dad says it'd get stolen or maybe I'd get hit by a car. What about you?"

"No, my mom said it would cost too much."

Arnold and Lewis were cousins who spent the month of July together each year—two weeks in the country with Arnold's family and the other two with Lewis's in the city. It was the only time they were together during the year and they crammed as much fun into each day as they could. Their tenth summer sticks in Arnold's memory. Born in the same year but four months apart, Arnold would hasten to make clear that HE was the senior cousin. They were allowed, for the first time, to roam the neighborhood without adult supervision. Their bodies were required in the kitchen at Lewis's home at precisely 6 PM; otherwise, tomorrow's activities would be severely curtailed.

One Saturday that summer they chose to explore a construction site nearby. They spent hours climbing the piles of re-rod and lumber, running through tunnels made by large drainage pipes and scrutinizing the backhoe and crane on site. All too soon it was time to start home. Arnold spotted an abandoned car left in the far corner of the site that had not yet been leveled. Not willing to pass up one final adven-

Mary Jane Mason
Larchmont, NY

ture, he climbed behind the wheel and became a Nascar driver. On the third lap, the yellow flag waved and on the fourth, the checkered flag. Lewis was yelling about their time limit. As he started to climb out, Arnold spotted a black sock. It looked too lumpy to be just an old sock. After a good shake, the sock yielded a Styrofoam cup with money in it. He stuffed it in his pocket and hurried over to meet Lewis.

"C'mon, we've really gotta hurry to get home on time," shot Lewis over his shoulder as they raced across the lot, out through the hole in the fence and down the street. At 6:01 PM, they closed the apartment door behind them and stood breathlessly in the kitchen. A long look from Lewis's mother put them on notice.

After washing up for dinner Arnold opened the styro cup and stared in wonder at the cash—more than he'd ever seen. Discarding the cup, he stuffed the bills deep into his jean shorts' pocket and went to dinner. Each bite of food was a large lump that wouldn't go down fast enough. Finally dinner was over, the evening board game and stories finished and he and Lewis were in bed and supposed to be sleeping.

"I think we can get our bikes now, Lewis."

"How?"

Arnold whispered, "I found a bunch of money in that old car today. I think there's enough so we can both get a bike."

Lewis was silent for a moment. "Whose money is it?"

"I don't know who left it there, but now it's ours. If they wanted it, they wouldn't have left it there."

"Why would somebody put their money in an old car like that?" Lewis asked suspiciously.

"I don't know," Arnold replied, "but who cares? It's ours now."

"I don't think we should take it," cautioned Lewis.

"C'mon Lewis," snorted Arnold, there's nothing wrong with it. There wasn't any name on it and it was just sitting there. I'm going to buy a bike when I go home."

"Okay Arnold, but I don't want the money. What if I got

Mary Jane Mason
Larchmont, NY

caught with all that money? I'd be in trouble. They'd say I stole it. Nope, you get your bike, but not me."

"Okay," sighed Arnold.

Several days after arriving home, Arnold went by the bike shop just to look. There was a sweet, blue, twelve speed Trek that he looked at longingly. It cost more than he had but next to it was a shiny, black Royce Union with off-road tires that was just right. He wished Lewis were there to see it.

Lewis. The thought of him reminded Arnold about who had left the money in the car. Maybe they would come looking for it and it wouldn't be there. Maybe it was money that the person was going to use for something special. Why had they left that money there? Maybe he shouldn't spend it? Well if he didn't spend it, what would he do with it?

Walking home from the bike shop, he passed the department store. One of the mannequins was wearing a lovely light green straw hat with a wide brim and a flowered scarf. How pretty it would look on his mother. Her birthday was in a couple of weeks. Tomorrow he would come back and buy that hat for her. She would wonder where he got the money for it. Oh! She would wonder where he got the money for the bike too. How would he explain that? So far, only Lewis knew about the money. Arnold was stuck. He had the money and knew how he wanted to spend it but he didn't feel good. What was wrong? The money had just been sitting there with nobody's name on it. He'd found it. What happened to finders keepers? Tomorrow he would get the hat and the bike. Then of course he'd have to tell where the money came from.

The next day he bought the hat. The saleslady wrapped it up very carefully and put it in a pretty shopping bag.

There was a crowd in the bike shop that day so Arnold looked around at the bikes and accessories while he waited. In one corner near the smaller sized bikes he saw a young boy crying as his mother tried to explain that the bike he wanted was just too expensive for her to buy. Arnold looked

Mary Jane Mason
Larchmont, NY

at the bike. He looked at the boy and his mother. He cast a long glance back at the Royce Union. He thought of his own mother in the lovely green hat and felt good. "Here," he said to the boy's mother, "I have this left over from buying my mother's birthday hat." He handed her the money, smiled and started home.

***

Sylvia Little-Sweat
Wingate, NC

Slant of Light

In evanescent
spring even the egret's cry
is hushed by the marsh.

Old Gullah women
arrange their sweet-grass baskets
to catch the morning.

Blackbirds in bare oaks
loudly cry *fire* then scatter
in burnt-orange skies.

A November moon
strings black opalescent pearls
on quicksilver sand.

Janice Babcock
Wauwatosa, WI

Thunder & Rumble

Thunder overhead
Angels bowling
Black clouds obliterate daylight

Neighbor's flag flaps in the turbulent wind
Torrents of rain fall
Thunder roars in the heavens

Train whistles warn of danger
Ambulance screams down State Street
Distant rumbling of Harleys mark their 110th Anniversary

Thunder yields to HOG rumble
Milwaukee miracle heartily welcomes Harley riders
110th celebration rev'ed up

Open road calls to riders and their angels
World countries were present with flags flying
Warriors roar down Wisconsin Avenue

International hard ride was worth it
Harley brotherhood crusade is alive
Steel stallions thunder and rumble forward

Peggy Trojan
Brule, WI

Photograph

Posed in the yard
Sophie, sitting, holding baby Ellen
husband Victor standing
wearing his suit jacket and good hat
hand on Wayne's shoulder.

My father, age four,
shirt buttoned to the neck
hair slicked, pants safety pinned
hiding a bit behind his mother's arm.
He looks intently into the camera lens
to what's coming.
Past losing his right eye when he is ten
past the 1918 Hinckley fire
that takes their house and cows
and burns his pet ram black,
into that most terrible part
when his dad dies
leaving all eight of them and Sophie
on the farm with no aid or money.
He is already sad.

He can't see just a little farther.
Far enough to see me
standing on the porch, waving.

Talking Stick 22, Fall 2013. Honors

Maureen Anaya
Berwick, ME

It's Never Too Late

Mable, an aging spinster, was surprised when she received a call from Roger stating he recently became a widower. Mable was still distraught over the loss of her sister, Barbara, whom gave her companionship for several years but recently lost her battle with cancer.

She remembered Roger from high school. At that time he was the love of her life; however, that would change when the draft came along and the Army sent him to Germany. Mable's heart sank when she received a letter from Roger stating he married a woman overseas who was pregnant.

Throughout the years, he periodically kept in touch by sending Christmas cards and one year a picture of his daughter. Mable felt as though life had passed her by even though she kept busy by volunteering for various activities.

Then, one day her doorbell rang and an elderly man stood in the doorway, holding a bouquet of roses. He slowly handed them to her and asked, "Am I still welcome in your life?"

Mable smiled as she replied, "Roger, come inside. It's never too late."

Lillian SMJ Saksek
Port Orange, FL

Not Even a Dash
In memory of Andreas & Catherine Suckfort 1755 — 1850

Dedicated to the thousands of early pioneers
that came in the 1700's to the wilderness we now call Maine.
They forged up waterery highways, cut down trees
from verdant forests with crude axes to build their log
       homes.
They prepared garden plots with simple hoes.
They carried water from the streams.
They lived in fear of Indian attacks, and often stared
       starvation in the face.
They fought the English and the French in order to keep their
       hard earned land,
yet they never doubted that they were where Almighty God
       wanted them to be.
They built churches and schools and helped one another
       build homes and barns.
They loved and produced offspring.
They danced and laughed and cried.
They worked hard and took pride in their accomplishments,
but now they lie in unmarked graves, except possibly for field
stones stuck up edgewise in each corner.
Generations to come would have lovely stones engraved with
       their names,
the date of their birth, **a dash**, and the date of their death.
Each dash representing a whole life lived. Each dash a silent
witness of agonies and joys, of drama untold.
Yet these dear, earlier courageous ones,
each life a story of its own,
Lay silent beneath the sod with, **"Not Even a Dash."**
But beyond the sunset in the archives of Heaven,
God has recorded every event of their lives, even as He is now
recording yours and mine.

Franklin Marshall
Simsbury, CT

A Doomsday Scenario for the 21st Century

Once in a while, when time, place and mood are just right, a critic will question whether I pointedly pursue a goal of inducing disquiet or depression in my readership. I submit that, dependent, of course, upon the acuteness of a reader's moral sensitivity, unrest or dejection emerges as the only credible or conceivable reaction to the business of my mind as it processes the stimuli emanating from a nightmare world in descent to a Gehenna of cultural and social decline inclusive of rudeness and incivility, of environmental havoc and wildlife extirpation, where last year Japanese fisheries killed in truly savage fashion 1092 whales of which 226 were pregnant, of atmospheric chemical defilement with banes like mercury and sulphur that befoul each human and faunal breath.

I propose that in modem times these insults to a respectful, if not always reverential, human habitation and to its sometimes manifested sense of stewardship have been and continue to be activated by a boundless, unabated, incorrigible corporate greediness that exploits the doggedly entrenched indifference of a self-absorbed public to the spoliation of the Earth's geologic and botanical treasury (Who cares, for example, should the Everglades become a limestone quarry with its panther population reduced to zero?), and that uses to their fullest the cash-acquisitive, yet Earth ravaging allowances flowing from an inordinately generous front of an ecologically obtuse political insanity.

The pillage, the plunder of sandstone plateaus, of greenwood watersheds, of riparian shallows will and must lead to the collapse of entire ecological systems with humankind in retroversion to a mode of tribal primitivism, where, as a byproduct of the rape of nature, the ugliness attendant upon land misuse and the lesions of extraction that scar a hither-

Franklin Marshall
Simsbury, CT

to unspoiled landscape rise to a peak of praiseworthiness within a society's hierarchy of aesthetic values, like however many paintings by Picasso that shall be viewed by as nothing more than variations on the theme of ugliness sophistically presented as an iconography deserving of salute by an authority covetous cognoscenti bearing an aggregate of testimonials to their putative critical acumen in matters of art, but, when applied to the science of bionomics, those obsequious, propagandist, largely inflated assessments throw off an oxymoron, where a deforested hence nude-ugly, acreage in Tasmania, say, or in the Amazon basin may be so rearranged rhetorically that it may be perceived as an exemplar for a beautiful landscape.

To engage the world is to grieve. The countryside vanishes. Rolling with gentle hill and dale impressions to a goldenrod horizon, a verdurous pasture quartering maybe a cow at rest beneath a cottonwood embranchment becomes a market place criss-crossed by features of commerce, like a pastry shop, a real estate brokerage house, a haberdashery. Once upon a quasi-rural time an owl hooted at twilight down a conifer aisle in anticipation of a rodent catch.

Since then, in less than a generation, a mixed business-residential geometry of big box squares and single homes, cookie-cutter circles displaces that erstwhile avian haunted pattern of pines, where the pop-pop-pop of a firearm discharging with serial certainty gives furtherance to the disrepute of a crime-eminent neighborhood—yes, the very neighborhood carved from that silvan sliver beloved by owls and boscage browsers.

In one of the cradles of civilization, warfare escapes the restraint of latency. May this conflict be seen as the precursor of a holocaust that spares no constituent of organic life together with its inorganic monuments? The world's population figures expand to the unprecedented reckoning that the Earth's resources requisite for the maintenance of any competent quality of life dwindle and dwindle and dwindle until

Franklin Marshall
Simsbury, CT

on one unfine morning following a cycle of barren diplomacy, a multiple of combatants hailing from an array of nations begin to contend, not for oil or religion, but for survival commodities, like water and grain.

On any number of occasions, I have given voice to this prospect, and if this picture of darksome death does not excite emotions of despair and rage, it should, because a funereal vision, promissory of dispread societal disorder and a radical, academically estimated decline in biodiversity, needs to be repainted; otherwise, a numerosity of floral and faunal species, many of which the human has not seen first hand, but which, in my opinion has as much of a right to life as the householders in an affluent, privileged enclave, like the gated and guarded *Harbor Heights*, falls into the canyon of casualty, and civilization races to ruin.

For the nonce though, as I sit on a late summer afternoon under my terrace umbrella reflecting upon the destiny of the world, three bumblebees intoxicate themselves with nectar weeping within the bells of hosta flowers, while overhead a hawk with motionless wings glides to the illusion of a firmamental zenith on currents of azure air.

***

Patrick T. Randolph
Kalamazoo, MI

Liquid Sky Fruit

Blueberry
      Summer skies
           Drip sweet raindrops.

Robert B. Moreland
Pleasant Prairie, WI

Flag Day

Dawn
sneaks in
the window
with a lake breeze.
She wakes cold, alone in the double bed.

Finest summer of two decades, share this
June together
yet apart,
longing
comes.

Flag
Day, who
remembers?
Place the colors
in the holder on garage's east side.

In a rush, like the breeze, remembers the
telephone call;
how he fought
for this
flag.

A
single
tear flows down
her cheek, ponders
how it could have been worse, he could have died.

Robert B. Moreland
Pleasant Prairie, WI

Sees his face, body without legs, staring
back, hope beyond
hope that healed,
they will
dance.

***

Mary Jo Balistreri
Genesee Depot, WI

On the Fourteenth Anniversary of Her Death
For my mother

At the end she sipped chamomile tea
    while Nat King Cole sang

Mostly silence filled her as June turned into December
    and dusk's matte shadows expanded along the ground

Blades of bone protruded through her thin apricot sweater
    and some days were one long nap

The more she lost the more she gave away
    watercolors copper enamels
  handmade quilts tap shoes and original routines

Tonight feathered wings brush across the sky
    wisps of purple-peach
        layered like the colors she painted on her canvas

There is nowhere I go she isn't

P. C. Moorehead
North Lake, WI

The Song

The river song ran through me
and sang the song it wanted to sing.

The river song ran through me.
I didn't know the melody or verse.

The river song ran through me,
creating itself, soothing me,
the river run.

***

Sylvia Little-Sweat
Wingate, NC

Pompeii

To walk alone at noon among the ruins
on cobble streets where ancient wheels
cut deeper ruts in stone is to hear again
the city's din—a wine vendor's cry,
a fountain's splash, the jostling of large
terra cotta jars in a passing cart, stark
laughter from a crowded shop or a sun-
filled atrium. To walk alone at noon
among the ruins is to taste the silence—
to taste volcanic ash that stopped
all mouths. To walk alone at noon
is to feel death's deepest, darkest mask.

Mary Ann Bedwell
Sedalia, MO

Endings

When our son died, he had been sick for over a year and the doctors had told us it was terminal. He was famine-thin, paralyzed from the upper chest on down and had lost most of his hair. We had hospice care to tell us what to expect.

My nephew's death, though, was different. He looked the picture of health: clear, ruddy complexion, muscular arms and chest, calloused hands. The heart monitor showed a steady beat and an even, normal blood pressure. His mother told me, however, the only part of his brain that was functioning was the part that was helping the breathing machine breathe for him.

His mother and father, his stepmother and stepfather, his aunt and uncle that had helped raise him, his two half-sisters, all the people who had been the closest to him, were there. All the people who were the most responsible and the most stricken by his condition. For Scott had been a problem almost from the time he was born.

Born in the seventies, he was introduced to the drug culture at an early age. His mother was from a family of alcoholics, which meant that not only were various family members users, they also enabled each other. Scott's mother and father divorced when he was a very small child and he was passed around among various family members. Being in a small town, this was easy, but Scott soon learned to play them off against each other to what he saw as his best advantage. He became a master manipulator, charming and spoiled; he basically directed his own upbringing.

This changed when his father remarried. His new stepmother had a daughter a little younger than Scott and she was concerned about Scott's influence on her. She also tried to maintain an orderly household and if there was anything that Scott wasn't, it was orderly. Scott's father didn't want

Mary Ann Bedwell
Sedalia, MO

to get involved in the battle so she became the wicked step-mother, the maker and enforcer of the rules. At one point Scott was sent to a children's home but his mother's sister petitioned to have him put in her care. Their family life-style was more relaxed and there was little conflict. He lived with them until he graduated from high school and seemingly thrived.

However, the basic problems were still there. He resented his father, still played his family members off against each other, and abused drugs and alcohol.

At one time he spent some time in prison. He was not welcome in his father's house.

"Poor Scott" was always the family problem, but a problem the family couldn't agree on how to handle. Some tried to organize the family to agree on a "tough love" policy; grandmothers wouldn't comply. Some saw drug and alcohol abuse as moral problems, others were enablers.

When I would ask about him, I would get a report based on the latest phone call. Scott had moved to Kansas City so family members rarely saw him but he did call occasionally. I last saw him six years ago when I was hosting the family Thanksgiving. He called me and asked if he could come, then left before most of the family arrived. He said he was going over to Aunt Vickie's, the aunt he had lived with during his school years. That was the last time I saw him before I went to Truman Medical Center yesterday.

Scott had been arrested Friday night, and put in jail. During the night, other inmates told jail attendants that he was on the floor. He was taken to the hospital and that was where I went yesterday. Scott looked better than I had seen him in a long time. He had worn his hair shaggy-long for years and had a full beard. They had cut his hair very short in the hospital and I could see his small, well-formed ears. Without all the loose hair, I noticed the long eyelashes and the small, straight nose. Family members held his hand and talked to him. Stories were told, most of them recounting

Mary Ann Bedwell
Sedalia, MO

some dare-devil escapade from his youth. Scott lay there, giving no indication that he was aware of any of this. His father and mother, in consultation with the doctor, had agreed that if he showed no signs of improvement by Sunday afternoon, they would remove the breathing machine.

I returned Sunday afternoon. The whole family was there, waiting for the emergency room doctor that had admitted him to issue the necessary orders. After a couple of hours the respiratory therapist came in and, asking us to step out of the room, removed all the apparatus except the heart monitor. It was left on so we could know exactly what was happening.

The therapist left, taking the breathing machine with her, and we returned to the room, accompanied by an RN and the chaplain. Scott continued to breathe for a few minutes, then just stopped. The heart monitors, which had been registering normal readings, began to fluctuate. The RN told us it was responding to the dropping of oxygen levels in the blood. At that point, most of us were crying. My twenty-two year old niece stood directly in front of me. I asked her if she wanted to stay; she indicated she did. We all held each other as the monitors gradually went blank. And it was done.

An autopsy had been scheduled, arrangements had been made for organs to be donated, the body would be cremated and a memorial service held for the family. This had all been decided by the two parents, who thankfully were in agreement on all points.

I agreed completely with all of their decisions but I do not know if I would have had the courage to follow through on them. This death should not have happened. At some point, someone should have done something differently. I am sure there was plenty of guilt in that room although none of it was mentioned. And there would have been no point to it. What was done was done and the people left have to live with each other. There would be no point in trying to assign blame— there was plenty of that during his lifetime.

Mary Ann Bedwell
Sedalia, MO

I mentioned our son's death. He died at home with his family who were comforted by the knowledge that everything that could have been done to make him well had been done. Scott died in the hospital surrounded by his family who had failed to do what was necessary for him. I felt like I had attended an execution.

***

Dawn Edwards
Ipswich, MA

Awaken Spring

Awaken Spring!
I am waiting
To catch the scent of daffodils,
To feel the warming showers,
To see returning robins
Preparing for their young.

Awaken Spring!
Oh, I am filled with
The beauty of a budding tree,
The smell of gentle breezes,
Remembering more carefree days
Of roller skates and kites.

Awaken Spring!
You are waiting
To make the grass grow green again,
To fill the air with laughter,
Don't wait too long, for now's the time
Awaken and begin.

M. F. Goode
Winchester, TN

The Smile

Think of a time when you felt stressed but had to continue on the errand you had begun. That was my situation one day as I uncurled myself from the front seat of my automobile in the parking lot of a large discount store. The auto was a fine one for driving, but it had bucket seats that positioned one's legs with a sharp angle at the hips. I was having a little trouble with my walking at that time and was annoyed at the awkwardness of getting out and ready to make my first steps toward the store entrance. My countenance probably displayed my displeasure as I moved forward slowly.

Focusing on my purpose for this trip to town, I was edging my way toward the door when I saw a young woman coming my direction with her loaded cart and stepping smartly in a purposeful way. She was neat and attractive and seemed to have had no problems with her shopping trip. As she came closer, she made eye-contact and gave me a warm, genuine *smile,* like she would give to a friend.

Even in my downcast mood, I recognized the smile as a special gift! I could hardly believe it! Immediately, I was relieved of my stressful feelings, like the sun had popped through on a dark cloudy day, warming my general feeling with its rays. I returned her smile, feeling the weight of bricks lift from my shoulders. Entering the store, I was able to enjoy my shopping as I filled my cart with supplies and items we needed at home. This good mood stayed with me for some time and I realized that we all are capable of helping others through simple deeds done in a caring way.

A warm gesture from a stranger gave me a satisfied feeling. It lifted my spirits and enabled me to continue throughout the days ahead. I resolved to be more ready to help others in stressful situations, realizing that a little smile was all it took to make me feel worthwhile!

George Wentz
Sturgeon Bay, WI

We Don't Talk About That

I was lucky to have a mother
when I was small
who told me secrets
about heaven and earth.

At sunset in the heat of August,
the sky turned red and she said
'twas the angels baking bread,
that's all.

The flash of lightening that lit the night
the burst of thunder that shook the house
was nothing more than angels bowling,
having fun.

A long time later when
the sound of trumpets played
I knew it was the angels,
calling me.

As the fog cleared
where I stood before the gate
I could smell the bread
and hear the rumble from afar.

Then I asked about my sins
and my guardian angel smiled
took me under her wing and said,
"We don't talk about that here."

Gertrude Durette
Bedford, NH

A Tribute to the Old Man of the Mountain
On the anniversary of his final crash into oblivion—
May 3, 2003

In the beautiful historical valley of Franconia Notch, in northern New Hampshire's White Mountains, the Old Man was viewed by countless millions of visitors during the eons of time after his creation.

The Old Man's stern face jutted boldly and precariously from the steep mountain face. His sharp eyes never missed returning the glance of an awe-inspired "looker." His alert countenance observed changes in nearby access roads. He never blinked at the multitude of cameras aimed at him over the years. This stunning, photogenic, stoic icon of New Hampshire's historical legacy seemed to be just "forever," so universally recognized, and such a joy to behold, with the backdrop of a brilliant blue sky. Why, then, did the sudden sad news of his final crashing end put us into such shocking disbelief and difficulty of acceptance?

It should have been a mere predictably tragic demise, sad but inevitable—which it was to those dedicated workers who crawled dangerously around the ancient facial features at necessary intervals, attempting to seal cracks in the visage, thus (hopefully) protecting Old Stoneface from the ravages of New Hampshire's severe winters. To most of us, though, the tragic crash of the stone structure was difficult to accept.

For years, a summer visit to see Old Stoneface was a lovely relaxing day for us, and bringing amazement and awe to our guests. We had picnics in the recreational area, followed by some spectacular photos of the structure.

After the crash, there was considerable discussion as to the cost, feasibility, and public reaction to any attempt to duplicate or replace the Old Man, and in what manner and where? Comments were invited from the general populace,

Gertrude Durette
Bedford, NH

and I chose to submit my feelings in poetic form, mailed in as suggested. I am pleased to repeat this little poem today (the words still fresh in my mind and also safely filed!):

> The Old Man of the Mountain—
> His memory we revere;
> Old Stoneface was on life support
> For many a painful year.
> We can't revive or save him;
> Our efforts now should cease,
> And let the Old Man fade away
> In dignity and peace.

***

Patrick T. Randolph
Kalamazoo, MI

6:00 a.m. Visit from Grandma K.

The voice of grandmother's smile
Meets my eyes,

Sending a grin deep down into
The song of my lips,
Into the music of my mind.

Dancing, dancing,
           Twirling
Toward
     the childhood of my bones.

Belva Ann Prycel
Alna, ME

The Waterman's Funeral

A Mainer lying in a church, a nave,
Still holds the echo of the ocean wave;
Upon his weathered hands or shuttered eyes,
Where blossoming waves could once devise
With sloopboat, schooner, or sable sea,
A salt-filled wide immensity.

Alluring undertones of ocean swells
That match the depths of the peeling bells;
With granite hardihood, aged toil,
He worked the rigors of the bay and soil;
Heard undulations of the coastal sea,
Saw birch tree shadows, and a host of free
And rock-made men, with seines or dredge,
And weirs to stretch from a tawny ledge;
Saw periwinkle that coats the ring
Of kelpweed, gathered in the early spring;
Or quickening autumns of battening tight
Before the cold-cast northern night—
The bell tolls louder, but cannot erase
The seared horizons of his ravaged face;
The waterman, who bears each crease and line
Of summit and seacoast, blood like brine.

Lorelee L. Sienkowski
Packwaukee, WI

Pico

She stands there at the door with confusion on her face.
She went there for a reason, but her memory has no trace.
Was she ready for the weather? Did she need to ring the
      bell?
Was she coming in from walking? Her mind has naught to
      tell.
She's ancient for her stature—big dogs don't last that
      long—
But slowly she's been aging, her hips are almost gone.
Her vet says "it's not fatal" just age and time and wear,
The only pains are walking, but she walks everywhere.
Her task has been protecting; the night's her shift to watch.
When people set their bedtime, she barks that she's THE
      BOSS.
She loves to sit in doorways, or on decks where she can
      see,
Or sometimes in the parlor, where she stands 'tween thee
      and me.
But nights are hard when we need sleep;
she needs to watch and rout.
We've moved into the parlor so that we can help her out.
We're closer to the doorway, our sleep is rearranged,
And weather's been so chilly, we cannot let her range.
We know one day she'll leave us for her eternal rest
But right now she's "our puppy" and such care for her is
      best.

Judith Wenzel Andersen
Owls Head, ME

Trying to Write

"Judy, you really should write." Hmmm...this from the man who feels anything out of place is a crisis, and does not hesitate to communicate the need to correct it immediately, and lives by the motto of his rugged Scottish Prep school— "There is more in you." Action is moving, not sitting. He feels that if not done now, the deed might never be done. He does not imply that I must be the fixer in chief, but there you are, interrupted yet again. I am irritated, do not jump up, believing firmly that there is no need to rush to clear the bathroom sink of the curlers, facial cleanser, cell phone, sun glasses, which admittedly belong someplace else, but will rest there perfectly well for a few more hours. Let me quickly tell you that I am a retired family doctor who believes that time can be a great healer, and while conservative in treating patients, I did not use this as an operating principle when the sick appeared with truly worrisome symptoms. My husband, on the other hand, a retired vascular and general surgeon, had to act immediately at the whiff of a ruptured aneurysm or cold leg. Thus, imagine our dialogues as I sit to write.

"There is no more somber enemy of good art than the pram in the hall," said Cyril Connelly—and I suspect He was talking about writers and artists who were male and did not want to be bothered by tots. Immense wealth and having no children would give one space. For the record, I would never have considered selling off my children. However, while juggling call schedule, office, insistent beeper, three children, and housework, I once (well, more than once) told my husband that all I wanted for Christmas was QUIET TIME AND A QUIET PLACE. Really.

Of course there are many solutions to finding a way and place to write. The "get up at 5:00 am, make a cup of coffee, and get going" school of thought seems drastic. Is it all it is

Judith Wenzel Andersen
Owls Head, ME

cracked up to be? Surely such writers must be living alone or have deep-sleeping partners not bothered by their excursions from the bedroom. Even then, being solitary in a room which needs lights because of the pre-sunrise darkness hovering outside, seems somehow sad. Don't they get hungry, sipping their coffee; what is their routine? I suspect it boils down to: (1) get up and make breakfast; (2) sit down again and eat; (3) open/close the door to let in/out the family pet; (4) sit down again and wonder about the weather; (5) fill the pet's food bowl; (6) watch the local weatherman on television; (7) on second thought, just take a peek at e-mail; (8) second cup of coffee, and that magic window slams shut, as it is time to start the day.

Some writers proudly manage, or say they do, by blast writing, using the twenty minutes free between putting the towels into the dryer and taking them out, or writing for the ten minutes that the cookies are baking. But, trust me, catastrophe looms. One somehow does not hear the kitchen timer until the smoke alarm dings and the firemen are at the door, or doesn't notice the two year old has discovered that liquid detergent makes fine sliding in the laundry room.

Of course, one does not have to be a mother to have problems settling down to write. I daydream and wonder what spinster Jane Austen did to write in her bustling household. She was excused from many household tasks by her family, but even with that, her letters describe a life of parties, visitors, family events, balls, dinner parties, teas, new clothes, gossip. A contemporary, Mrs. Mitford, described her as "the prettiest, most affected, husband-hunting butterfly she ever remembers." In retrospect, her time or inclination to sit quietly seems rather limited. Indeed, visiting her home in Chawton, where she apparently revised several of her books in her later years, one sees a simple table and chair by the window where she wrote, with a great view of the road and the very distracting comings and goings of her neighbors. She did go so far as to hide out in her changing room from

Judith Wenzel Andersen
Owls Head, ME

time to time, not allowing a squeaky door to be repaired so that she could hear anyone approaching and hide her manuscripts.

And what of Ernest Hemingway, with whom I share a fragile link? We both grew up in Oak Park, Illinois, and separated by several generations, shared the demanding Mr. John Gehlmann who was student newspaper advisor for Ernie, and English teacher for me. Dirty Ernie earned his nickname by publishing a renegade journal of salacious jokes on the sly which was confiscated by the principal, a truly horrific deed in our tea-totaling, Victorian village at the time. He was not expelled, thanks to Mr. G.'s intervention. At the beginning of his freewheeling lifestyle, the budding bad boy writer did not seem to need peaceful contemplation. According to George Plimpton, the older Hemingway, did nevertheless organize a rigid schedule of writing. He typed standing looking at the wall "all morning in oversized loafers on the worn skin of a lesser kudu" with a reward at the end, described by Papa himself as "done by noon and drunk by three."

Where else and how else can one write? Great authors have needed help in settling down to their work. Edith Wharton, Winston Churchill, and Mark Twain loved the silence and calm of the bath tub. Agatha Christie improved the venue by soaking in the bubbles, eating apples. Truman Capote wrote lying down with a cup of tea, and later with a sherry, progressing to a martini. Balzac drank fifty cups of coffee a day to stir his juices, while slow-going Proust began the day with coffee, croissants, and opium.

Perhaps the most interesting advice about the best place to write came from Dorothy Parker, who said: "in your head." Okay!

Excuse, me. The phone just rang, the washing machine beeped, and my husband walked into the kitchen wondering when lunch would be ready. Let's explore this further when we have some quiet time in our heads.

Diane H. Schetky
Topsham, ME

Waiting for the Bus

The kids were getting restless
waiting for the bus that would
take them from the city to
upstate New York.

They were dressed in their best
as if going to church.
Sadie clung to her mother's
shiny black, plastic pocketbook
and looked up at the bright
lights in the bus terminal.

Ella tried to soothe her crying
baby and Sadie kept asking
"Mama, when we gonna
see Papa?"

Ella's husband, Devon, had
been transferred from
Riker's Island to a prison
way up north.

She'd not told Sadie where
he was or why, as how could
a child so young understand?

Ella, herself, didn't really
understand what made
him do it and why he
got such a long sentence.

Diane H. Schetky
Topsham, ME

She'd never been out of the city,
didn't know what to expect and
worried how the kids would
do on the six hour bus ride.

She wondered why she'd
stood by her man and
how much longer
she could cope on her own
and afford the bus fare.
She fought back a tear
so as not to upset her children.

***

Barbara J. Dorner
DePere, WI

We Pledge Our Allegiance

We pledge our allegiance to the heroes of war,
Who have marched into battle defending our shore,
Who have died for our factories our homes and our farms,
Who have fought for the truth and our right to bear arms,
To those brave men and women who gave up their lives,
For our sons and our daughters, our husbands and wives,
By the land, by the air, by the spacious blue sea,
To The Soldiers That Keep Our America free!

Patricia Foldvary
Wauwatosa, WI

A Deeper Shade of Melancholy

Set back from the road
it stands a-tilt like a tipsy bar patron
weathered past peeling.

Barely visible gravel suggests a drive
trailing off the hard road along vestiges
of rotted wood fence.

Low sun glitters on one cracked glass eye
that blinks shut as rays slip beyond the hill.
Half-dead branches stirred by fickle
breezes bounce like fluttering lashes.

Whose children chased through the door
now hanging askew?
What animals warmed the ghostly barn?

The story of a time of purpose
like that of an old man
hides in the shell of what once was.
None remain to tell it.
Earth patiently waits.

Milton M. Gross
Ellsworth, ME

Down the Road a Piece
Where have all those quiet, rustic paths gone?

My wife and I once visited the old Robert Frost farm in New Hampshire and were intrigued when we followed the old farm road into the woods and came to the fork in the road. The road less traveled.

Actually, we prefer those less traveled paths to the highways leading the masses to the mall.

After I return from a difficult hike, I find myself yearning for a quiet, rural pathway down which I can just amble. The peacefulness of such scenes at times overwhelms me, and when life brings stress my way I tend to close my eyes and picture myself on such a path.

My little philosophical dilemma has to do with Maine history. The Native Americans living here or there decided to go there or somewhere for this or that reason. The Maineac claim that "you can't get theyah from heah" had not dawned on these People of the Dawn, so they got somewhere from somewhere else. They did it, of course, by canoe.

But they also walked—something from which modern Maineacs and other Americans could profit regarding emotional and physical health.

Those walks tended to be over the easiest routes, those folks not looking for the mountain or "wilderness" adventure so many of us seek today in our hiking.

Then along came Mr. European, who, of course, had all the answers to life, a really big canoe with sails, boots that could protect their feet much better than those Native American moccasins, and wheelbarrows and hand carts with which they could tote stuff they had to tote.

So their boots tromped down those Indian paths and turned them to mud. Then the resourceful Europeans in their quest to get places overland followed those paths, which

Milton M. Gross
Ellsworth, ME

meant the paths had to be widened a bit for their horses. Next came the two-wheeled cart, then the wagon, which required widening those paths more. Now those paths were called roads.

These roads had problems, such as the persistent Maine mud and snow in winter. The mud they just wallowed through, boots, horses, wagons, and all. The snow they learned to mash down and harden with devices pulled by horses, so sleighs could more easily glide over them.

And these problems were worse when those first horse-less buggies arrived. They got stuck and had to be pulled out of the mud by those horses.

So the badly eroded roads were paved. No doubt these modern "trails" are a lot easier to drive on and get us there so much faster so we can do....now what was it that we all rushed down that paved highway to do and got there so much sooner? But I have never stood alongside a highway, breathed deeply, and become awestruck by the silence and fresh air.

Several years ago the feds passed a law requiring that when trails near roads were repaired or updated, they also were to be made handicap accessible. So handicapped-friendly improved trails replaced what had been a path.

Will our quiet places someday become paved highways? If they do, where will I find a quiet country lane on which to ramble while I'm thinking about this dilemma.

All this thinking about hiking on the less traveled way may be too much for me, because I feel like I need to get out of the house and go for a nice walk along a quiet path. Thankfully, there are still several nearby.

Sherry Ballou Hanson
Portland, OR

Stonehenge by Cab

British Airways did a nice job: wine with dinner, soft booties, even a tiny toothbrush and tube of paste. After watching the virtual globe on the seat backs in front of us and being mesmerized by that arrow creeping across "the pond," my sister and I dozed, not real sleep, but then we landed on another continent and forgot about being tired.

She and I spent a couple of days in London, walking along the Thames checking out the statuary and the Mariners' Memorial, and visiting the buildings at the Tower of London. In the Beauchamp Tower we were overwhelmed by the despair evident in many of the messages scratched into walls. In a small alcove one of the Beefeaters showed us a tiny carving of Jesus on a cross carved into the wall. Later we cringed at the ingenious devices of torture of the day, including the axe and the block. We watched the changing of the guard at Buckingham Palace and finally boarded a train at Victoria Station and left the city for Salisbury.

Sheep grazed in the rich green fields unrolling outside our passenger windows and the occasional crumbling castle passed by. It began to rain, and by the time we arrived in Salisbury and engaged a cab to take us to our little inn it was pouring down buckets. We feared for our next day's journey out to Stonehenge, especially since there was no regular bus service into town. It happened that the brother of our innkeeper was the cabbie who had delivered us the day before and he was glad to come back and take us out to the enigmatic circle of stones. He had done this a few times before, even hauling groupies out for rock concerts at the monument "in the day." No more. Time and erosion have taken their toll and individuals with chisels have excised chunks from the sarsen stones. It is also suspected that construction projects in generations past made off with good-

Sherry Ballou Hanson
Portland, OR

sized pieces of broken pillars.

Today's equinox and solstice gatherings are a far cry from the New Age orgies of the 1970s, let alone ancient pagan and druid rituals that must have accompanied burials on the site. You cannot walk among the arches anymore, and the remnants of bluestones brought all the way from Wales by land and sea 2,600 years before Christ are off limits.

Clouds still hung heavy when our driver arrived early in the morning to pick us up. We took our backpacks and hopped in the cab, hoping for the best, but make no mistake; we were going out there to the Salisbury Plain rain or shine.

After a few tales from his days as a young fan when groups such as U2 rocked the night out on the downs, our driver went silent. As the road straightened ahead a faint orange glow ignited on the horizon and then I saw it, still a few miles away, tiny and intricate from this distance, a geometric pattern of stones rising from the plain and I knew no god had made this. Only humans build arches, and on the great sweep of the Wiltshire Downs they were surprisingly small from our perspective three miles out.

I guess I had simplistic expectations that all of a sudden I would fetch up at this great tower of stones. Maybe from another direction, or on a bus full of tourists, but not the way we came, in a cab across the downs to this temple of gods, or is it a path to the equinox?

Six years later that picture of Stonehenge is still etched on my brain. Stone took over from wood more than 2,000 years ago, which followed the first constructions on the site: earthworks used as burial sites hundreds of years before any other structures were built there. My sister and I had the same questions: Who built these trilithon arches and how did they know to carve the lintels to sit securely on top of the sarsen stones? That requires a tongue and groove fitting and where did they learn that? This question had a special intensity for us, as our ancestors who emigrated from England in the 1620s came from this plain. Were they here in this space

Sherry Ballou Hanson
Portland, OR

thousands of years ago and might we truly be descended from those people?

I felt drawn to this place and the closer I got to the stones, the stronger the pull. Gradually, I became aware of a steady hum, a feeling like electricity running through the ground on which I stood. My sister and I were the first arrivals, but then came the buses and I already had this feeling that we had crossed a sort of bridge: there is before Stonehenge and there is after. It's in the blood now.

We stayed on viewing the arches from every angle; we took pictures to prove we had been there, as if we needed proof. Eventually we visited the tiny shop for a souvenir and a cup of coffee. We sat out on the grass and I wondered if this steady hum was our ancestors speaking across the ages.

Like many of the world's stone megaliths, Stonehenge is aligned with the setting sun at midwinter. This is obviously not by accident and the purpose may have been to serve as a calendar to let people know when it would next be safe to plant their crops. Numerous burial chambers on the site were oriented with a shaft that allowed the sun to reach the interior only at midwinter. These people may have hoped their dead might rise again as their crops would. I'm still wondering what my ancestors were saying.

Thomas Peter Bennett
Bradenton, FL

Past Present

After the rain,
I loll in the squelchy
grass, roll over to
wash away the sweat of
an afternoon digging for
clay-encrusted fossils.

A flash erupts in the
leaden sky, followed by
a thunder cymbal and
a distant drum roll,
the same sound heard
when ancient creatures,
lolled in the grass
after the rain.

***

Lichen Repast

After the rain,
the ground was garnished
with twigs and branches,
seasoned with yellow, gray
and leathery splotches of
primeval plant life—a
banquet for beetles and slugs.

Thomas Peter Bennett
Bradenton, FL

Millipede Mystery

After the rain,
millions of legs
tramp from leaf litter
down to the pond.
Hours later, a multitude of
death-coiled millipedes floated
bloated on the pond surface.
Was it the rain?

***

After the Rain

Is a wonderful
time for loving
as every chartreuse
tree frog knows.

Thomas Peter Bennett
Bradenton, FL

Gargoyles of the Pond

After dark,
after the rain,
frog sentinels
align pond side
and begin their grunting guard.
Gargoyle still, they
survey a film of fog
rising from the pond's skin.
Some croak, then dive
into the dark unknown.
On-shore sentinels
croak approval.

***

Patricia Foldvary
Wauwatosa, WI

Just One Day

There comes a day—just one day—
when late winter takes a breath.
Icicles give themselves up one drip at a time.
Nostrils sense spring's faint tease.
The teenager jogs by in shorts and T-shirt.
Pale green shoots—last week asleep
under a snowy coverlet—stretch upward.
We know it's too soon
but like cats at the sound of the can opener
we come running and open our windows.

Robert Erickson
Round Pond, ME

Winter

My mind peers out on ultimate grey
If snow and cold could talk, they'd say
"This is winter, so cold and bleak
With wind and slush; misery I speak"

Peering again on the harbor round
Grey ocean to grey shore out to the sound
My frigid soul cries out in abject thirst
For the soothing warmth of an August First

***

Peggy Trojan
Brule, WI

Treasure

In my summer heart
I precious tucked
my thoughts of you.
They warm me still
like sun on my back
when wind blows
cool lake shivers
on my skin.

Liz Moser
Baltimore, MD

Run

Run, run
Run to win, to stay ahead
Run for reelection
Run a race
Run a stocking
Run a motor
Run toward warmth and morning light
Run toward dark and lover waiting
Run away from home
Run from someone that you've hurt
Run from pain
Run, run
till breath is gone
till legs give way.

Don't look back.

Janice Babcock
Wauwatosa, WI

Auschwitz

It was a gray and rainy September day that I first went to Auschwitz. I knew a bit about the Nazi death camps, but didn't know exactly what I was going to be exposed to on the tour.

I knew that millions of Jews were killed by the Nazis in the Holocaust. I knew that a smaller number of others were killed by the Nazis in the Holocaust. I knew that Auschwitz was one of the major killing camps. I knew that I would see the barracks in Auschwitz and nearby Birkenau, Poland. I knew I would see barbed wire surrounding the camp and the many cell blocks. I knew the prisoners were told to take off their clothing, hang them on hooks outside the shower room and walk in naked. I knew that prisoners were told to remember their hook number, suggesting they would return alive to retrieve their personal effects. I knew that in the gas room ceiling there were fake shower heads which really spread the poisonous vapor. I knew that I would see the tubes on the roof that looked like chimneys, but really carried the poisonous gas to the prisoners in the shower room. I knew that I would see the crematories that were used to burn the bodies.

I did not know that the second highest number of people murdered by the Nazis were Gypsies. I did not expect to see the huge number of barracks in Auschwitz and Birkenau. I did not expect to see relatively tiny stalls that housed dozens of prisoners in the top and bottom of the barracks in Birkenau. I did not expect to hear that rats would nibble on the prisoners' feet that were unfortunate to be at the bottom of the lower stall. I did not know that the heating stoves in the original Polish military barracks would never be used to provide even a little heat for the prisoners in the winter. I did not know that the some of the bathrooms or disinfection

Janice Babcock
Wauwatosa, WI

rooms could hold hundreds to a thousand people at a time, to be murdered with Zyklon B poison gas. I did not know that the Nazi soldiers witnessed the extermination through a special locked window. For some victims, dying could last up to 20 minutes. I did not know that the Auschwitz and Birkenau ovens were used to burn several corpses at a time. I did not know that to handle the volume at the Holocaust's height, this burning went on continuously day and night. I did not know that Jewish boys operated the incinerator ovens. They were called the "special squad" and were housed separately from the other inmates. I did not know that their life expectancy was only a few weeks to a few months. Then they were shot, so no survivors could document the cremation of the bodies with those ashes spread as fertilizer or filling material to build roads.

I learned of the plunder taken from the innocent dead prisoners: local currency, bank notes, wedding rings, jewelry, watches and other precious items. Fingers were cut off to remove the rings. These personal items from some of the millions of victims made them very real people to me. I was aghast!

Nothing could have prepared me for seeing all of the huge floor-to-ceiling enclosed cases holding hundreds of the items. This made the Holocaust alive to me.

We were told that some of the prisoners were allowed to bring luggage when snatched from their towns and villages. They were shoved into locked cattle cars for days to a week or more with no food or liquid, unless they brought some. Only a bucket was available for excrement. Train travel time depended on which European country they came from.

That would explain why the first display I saw was piles of luggage. The suitcases were carefully labeled with people's names and addresses. One pharmacist clearly indicated that his luggage contained pharmaceutical supplies.

The next display had all different kinds, colors and shapes of women's shoes. Another was filled to the brim with

Janice Babcock
Wauwatosa, WI

glasses.

I saw a display with all types of prosthetic legs and arm braces that the victims had worn. The crippled were immediately destined for death.

One of the displays that was the most difficult for me to witness was the one holding women's hair either cut off after they were gassed or shaved off when their ID number was burned into their arm. We were told the hair was spun into thread and turned into felt for the war industry, for clothing, mattresses, or other things.

We were told that the storage buildings on the grounds in Camp Jargon were called "Canada." That country was thought to be prosperous. This housed valuable booty like gold teeth that the Nazis extracted, jewelry, household goods, dishes, tableware, cooking pots, all sizes of knives, silver candlesticks, clocks and other things of value.

The plunder taken from the Jews, Gypsies, and other people from all the European countries involved in the Holocaust was doled out to the officers, their girlfriends, the Reich Youth Leadership, Luftwaffe pilots, U-boat crews or recycled back into Germany. In the entire Holocaust, about six million Jews and five million others were killed.

While on this tour, our guide was excellent in putting the "human touch" to the killing of millions of Jews and European people. I listened intently, observed and pondered my own thoughts of the tragedy that we were seeing before us. My stomach often knotted up learning in detail of the Nazi extermination methods and those millions of desecrated corpses. I was aghast! I saw a large glass container holding human ashes representing those millions.

I didn't hear anyone say a word.

It was a gray rainy day for me.

First published in *Inspiration Café,* Volume 16, Number 2, Waukesha County Technical College, Pewaukee, WI.

GOOSE RIVER ANTHOLOGY, 2015

We seek selections of fine poetry, essays, and short stories (3,000 words or less) for the 13th annual *Goose River Anthology, 2015*. The book will be beautifully produced with full color cover and full color dust jacket for hard covers.

You may submit even if you have been published before in a previous edition of the *Goose River Anthology*. We retain one-time publishing rights. All rights revert back to the author after publication. You may submit as many pieces as you like.

EARN CASH ROYALTIES. Author will receive a 10% royalty on all sales that he or she generates.

There is no purchase required and nothing is required of the author for publication. Deadline for submissions is March 31, 2015. Publication will be in the fall of 2015 (they make great Christmas gifts). Guidelines are as follows:

- Submit clean, typed copy by snail mail—**mandatory**
- Email a Word or rtf file to us (if possible)
- Reading fee: $1.00 per page
- Do not put two poems on the same page
- Essays and short stories should be double-spaced
- SASE for notification (one forever stamp) plus additional postage for possible return of submission if desired.
- Author's name & address at top of each page of paper copy and first page of emailed copies.

Submit to:
Goose River Anthology, 2015
3400 Friendship Road
Waldoboro, ME 04572-6337
E mail: gooseriverpress@roadrunner.com
www.gooseriverpress.com